SUN GODS AND SACRIFICE

PHILIP STEELE
FIONA MACDONALD

southwater

This edition is published by Southwater

Southwater is an imprint of Anness Publishing Ltd
Hermes House, 88–89 Blackfriars Road
London SE1 8HA
tel. 020 7401 2077; fax 020 7633 9499
www.southwaterbooks.com; info@anness.com

UK agent: The Manning Partnership Ltd
tel. 01225 478444; fax 01225 478440;
sales@manning-partnership.co.uk

UK distributor: Grantham Book Services Ltd
tel. 01476 541080; fax 01476 541061;
orders@gbs.tbs-ltd.co.uk

North American agent/distributor:
National Book Network
tel. 301 459 3366; fax 301 429 5746;
www.nbnbooks.com

Australian agent/distributor: Pan Macmillan Australia
tel. 1300 135 113; fax 1300 135 103;
customer.service@macmillan.com.au

New Zealand agent/distributor: David Bateman Ltd
tel. (09) 415 7664; fax (09) 415 8892

Publisher: Joanna Lorenz
Managing Editor: Helen Sudell
Editor: Joy Wotton
Designers: Caroline Reeves, Margaret Sadler,
 Sarah Williams
Illustration: Rob Ashby, Julian Baker, Vanessa Card,
 Stuart Carter, Stephen Gyapay, Clive Spong
Photography: John Freeman
Production Controller: Darren Price

Anness Publishing would like to thank the following
children for modelling for this book: Jake Lewis
Courtney Andrews, Anthony Bainbridge, Sabirah
Bari, Patrick Clifford, Molly Cooper, Daniel Djanan,
Ricky Garrett, Sasha Haworth, Jodie King, Alex
Lindblom-Smith, Lucy Nightingale, Ifi Obi, Graham
Oppong, Joshua Adam Laidlaw Parkin, Mai-Anh
Peterson, Adrianne S. Punzalan, Charlie Ray, Katie
Louise Stevens, Samantha Street, Reece Warman,
Joseph Williams.

Previously published in two separate volumes, *Step Into
the Aztec & Maya Worlds* and *Step Into the Inca World*

10 9 8 7 6 5 4 3 2 1

CONTENTS

Introduction

BEFORE EUROPEANS ARRIVED in 1492, America was home to many astonishing civilizations. Among the greatest were those created by the Maya, Aztec and Inca peoples. The Maya lived in the hills and valleys of Mesoamerica – the narrow strip of land where North and South America meet. They ruled strong kingdoms from around AD300 to 900. The Aztecs were based in the far north of Mesoamerica, in the land known today as the Central Valley of Mexico. They were most powerful from 1325 to 1519. The Incas lived in the Andes mountains and ruled a vast empire from around 1100 to 1532, stretching the length of South America.

WONDERFUL WEAVERS
The Incas wove complex textiles using backstrap looms. The warp threads were held between a post and a beam attached to the weaver's waist.

EARLY ANCESTORS

The history of the Maya, Aztecs and Incas begins some time between 40,000 and 20,000BC. Groups of hunter-gatherers walked from Siberia to North America over a land-bridge (strip of land) left uncovered by low sea-levels during the last Ice Age. Very slowly, the settlers spread southwards to different parts of the continent, reaching Mesoamerica by around 12,000BC and the tip of South America by around 8000BC.

EARLY WRITING
The first-known Maya writing was produced in around 292BC. They used picture-symbols and sound-symbols.

EXTREME ENVIRONMENTS

These first settlers found themselves living in difficult conditions. Mesoamerica, where Maya and Aztec civilizations developed, has hot, humid rainforests, dry, sun-baked valleys, and towering volcanoes. The west of South America, home of the Inca Empire, has the longest stretch of mountains in the world – the high Andes mountains – densely forested foothills, and a salty desert strip along the coast.

WATER ROADS
The Maya, Aztecs and Incas had no wheeled transport. Boats and rafts travelled on lakes, rivers and the sea, and porters carried heavy loads.

FRUITS OF THE DESERT
Cacti thrive in Mesoamerica's dry semi-desert. The sap is made into a drink and the fibres into clothing.

FARMING COMMUNITIES

The early settlers survived by catching wild animals and by fishing, or by gathering wild berries, nuts and roots. After around 3000BC, they discovered how to plant seeds and grow food. They began to build houses in villages, and, later, to cut terraced fields in steep hillsides and plan irrigation schemes to bring water to vegetable gardens. Their crops included some of the modern world's favourite foods – potatoes from the Andes mountains, tomatoes and chillies from the dry lands of Mesoamerica, and cocoa, which was used to make chocolate, from Mesoamerican rainforests.

AZTEC SETTLERS
In around AD1100, Aztecs left the dry semi-desert in northern Mexico and went south to find a new place to live.

Early American craftworkers also began to develop useful skills, weaving cloth, shaping stone and making pottery. They traded these craft goods with neighbouring peoples for other useful items, or food. They also used their craft skills to express their religious beliefs. They made precious items to leave at holy places, to please the gods, and created images of nature gods, such as the Sun and Moon, or magic animal spirits, such as monkeys and jaguars.

GOLDEN FACE
The Chimu, Incas and other peoples of South America made face-masks of gold to lay on the faces of the dead.

CLANS, TRIBES AND CULTURES

Over the centuries, the early Americans also organized themselves into many separate clans and tribes. They began to follow strong leaders, who recruited armies to defend their settlements or conquer more land. Leaders also made rules for how society should be run, and how wealth and power should be shared.

Slowly, separate tribes developed their own special cultures and lifestyles. Although their political power often did not last long, their ideas, inventions, discoveries, myths, legends and artistic styles were all handed down to later civilizations, including the Maya, Aztecs and Incas, and helped to make them great.

MASK OF DEATH
Lord Pacal, ruler of the Maya city of Palenque, was buried wearing a mask of green jade in a pyramid-shaped temple. Only the very richest city-states had the wealth to bury their rulers like this.

SECRETS OF THE PAST
This stone figure from Oaxaca was carved by a sculptor from one of the ancient civilizations that flourished in Mesoamerica.

SHARED HERITAGE

The Maya, Aztec, and Inca civilizations were separated from each other in time, and by long distances and difficult terrain. Their languages and customs were very different. Yet – like other ancient Mesoamerican peoples, including the Olmecs and the Toltecs – because they were based on earlier American traditions, they had much in common.

All three civilizations were well organized and strictly controlled. Their men served the State by fighting in the army. Well-trained government officials from all three civilizations kept detailed records of royal reigns, battles and taxes. Maya and Aztec scribes developed the first systems of writing in America.

Expert craftworkers in Maya, Aztec and Inca lands built splendid cities, with temples, palaces and markets, and made wonderful clothes, jewellery, and luxury household goods, which only the wealthiest members of society could enjoy. Most important of all, in their own view, Maya, Aztec and Inca people shared many religious beliefs about life and death, gods and sacrifices.

STONE WARRIOR
The Toltec people lived in central Mexico. Their soldiers were famous for their battle skills.

MASTERS OF STONE
The Temple of the Warriors at Chichen-Itza was built by the Maya. It is an almost exact replica of one built by the Toltecs at Tula, which shows how one culture can influence another.

HUMAN SACRIFICE
This stone statue is carrying a dish in his arms. It may have been used to hold blood or hearts from human sacrifices made by the Aztecs.

LIFE AND DEATH

The Maya, Aztecs and Incas all believed that the world was made by a powerful creator – whom the Incas called Wiraqocha, the "old man of the sky". But in many ways, the gods of the Sun, Moon and the weather were more important to most early Americans. These nature gods brought warmth, light, rain and the promise of a good harvest. Without their help, many people would die. To please these gods, the Maya, Aztecs and Incas offered them gifts of the most precious things they owned – gold or their own children. The Aztecs sacrificed many prisoners since they believed that their gods had to be fed with human hearts and blood, or else the world would come to an end.

GOD-LIKE POWERS

The Maya, Aztec and Inca lands were all governed by strong rulers, who claimed kinship with the gods. The Incas believed that their rulers were descended from Inti, the God of the Sun. Maya kings added the name for the Sun god, Kinich, to their own royal titles, and Aztec rulers were often portrayed dressed as gods with beautiful clothes and jewellery.

Rulers also had important religious responsibilities. Maya kings and queens pierced their own flesh and offered their blood to the gods, and the Inca *Willak Umu* (high priest) was always a member of the royal family.

REACHING FOR THE SKY
The Maya, Aztecs and Incas built tall pyramid temples reaching up to the sky, home of the sun god. Their builders worked without metal tools.

FINE FEATHERS
Aztec rulers, nobles and warriors wore splendid costumes highly decorated with brightly coloured feathers.

CONQUEST, COLLAPSE – AND SURVIVAL

In the year 1500, the Maya, Aztec and Inca civilizations seemed secure and confident. But within a few years, all three were facing disaster. Spanish soldiers invaded Aztec lands in 1519, and conquered them two years later. Maya states were overpowered by Spain in 1542. The Inca Empire collapsed in 1536, and the last Inca ruler was killed in 1572. By 1600, over half of all Maya, Aztec and Inca people had died – mostly from European diseases, introduced by the conquerors.

Today, the ruins of great Maya, Aztec and Inca cities are mostly buried under modern buildings or overgrown by trees and creepers. The treasures they once contained have been removed or destroyed. But enough evidence survives to give us some idea of their achievements. Millions of their descendants still live in the lands their ancestors once ruled. They speak modern forms of their old languages, and keep many of their beliefs and traditions alive.

WARRIORS FROM SPAIN
The Spanish conquest of the 1600s was a disaster for all native Americans. Millions were killed or became slaves.

DESCENDANTS OF THE EMPERORS
The felt hats, handwoven cloaks, handmade baskets and goods on sale in this modern-day market in Ecuador link the past with the present.

7

Aztecs and Maya

The Maya and the Aztecs were proud and powerful peoples who ruled magnificent city states in ancient Mesoamerica. They worshipped the same family of gods, built tall pyramid temples and practised human sacrifice. Their craftworkers created wonderful objects from gold, feathers and stone. Their priests were great astronomers, and their scribes invented the first writing systems in America, using picture-symbols. The Aztecs and Maya grew rich through trading and collecting tribute from conquered peoples.

Great Civilizations

The Aztecs lived in Mesoamerica — the region where North and South America meet. It includes the countries of Mexico, Guatemala, Honduras, El Salvador and Belize. During the past 3,000 years, Mesoamerica has been home to many great civilizations, including the Olmecs, the Maya, the Toltecs and the Aztecs. The Aztecs were the last of these to arrive, coming from the north in around AD1200. In about 1420 they began to conquer a mighty empire. But in 1521 they were themselves conquered by Spanish soldiers, who came to America in search of gold. Over the next hundred years, the rest of Mesoamerica also fell to the Spaniards.

Even so, the descendants of these cultures still live in the area today. Many ancient Mesoamerican words, customs and beliefs survive, as do beautiful hand-painted books, mysterious ruins and amazing treasures.

OLMEC POWER
This giant stone head was carved by the Olmecs, the earliest of many great civilizations that flourished in Mesoamerica. Like the Maya and Aztecs, the Olmecs were skilled stone workers and built great cities.

UNCOVERING THE PAST
This temple is in Belize. Remains of such great buildings give archaeologists important clues about the people who built them.

TIMELINE 5000BC–AD800

Many civilizations were powerful in Mesoamerica at different times. The Maya were most successful between AD600–900. The Aztecs were at the height of power from AD1428–AD1520.

5000BC The Maya settle along the Pacific and Caribbean coasts of Mesoamerica.

2000BC People begin to farm in Guatemala, Belize and south-east Mexico.

Olmec figure

2000BC The beginning of the period known as the Preclassic era.

1200BC Olmec people are powerful in Mesoamerica. They remain an important power until 400BC.

1000BC Maya craftworkers begin to copy Olmec pottery and jade carvings.

900BC Maya farmers design and use irrigation systems.

600BC The Zapotec civilization begins to flourish at Monte Alban.

Maya codex

300BC The Maya population starts to grow rapidly. Cities are built.

292BC The first-known Maya writing is produced.

150BC–AD500 The people living in the city of Teotihuacan grow powerful.

AD250 The beginning of the greatest period of Maya power, known as the Classic Maya era. This lasts until AD900.

mask from Teotihuacan

5000BC   2000BC   300BC   AD500

THE GREAT TEMPLE

The Maya built this pyramid at Chichen-Itza in south-eastern Mexico, around AD1000. Historians believe that the Putun people may also have established themselves at Chichen-Itza. The pyramid was designed so that twice a year the Sun casts a snake-shaped shadow down the steps. Buildings like this tell us about the religious beliefs of the Maya and also show what skilful builders they were. Maya and Aztec stone masons worked without the help of metal tools.

THE FACE OF A GOD

This mask represents the god Tezcatlipoca. It is made of pieces of semi-precious stone fixed to a real human skull. Masks like this were worn during religious ceremonies, or displayed in temples as offerings to the gods.

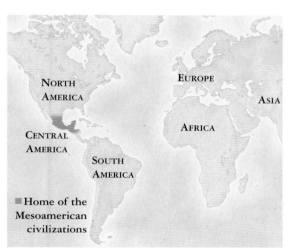

NORTH AMERICA

EUROPE

ASIA

AFRICA

CENTRAL AMERICA

SOUTH AMERICA

■ Home of the Mesoamerican civilizations

MESSAGES IN CODE

These are Aztec picture-symbols for days, written in a folding book called a codex. Mesoamerican civilizations kept records of important people, places and events in picture-writing.

MESOAMERICA IN THE WORLD

For centuries, Mesoamerica was home to many different civilizations, but there were links between them, especially in farming, technology and religious beliefs. Until around AD1500, these Mesoamerican civilizations had very little contact with the rest of the world.

AD550 This is the time of the Maya's greatest artistic achievements. Fine temples and palaces in cities such as Kabah, Copan, Palenque, Uxmal and Tikal are built. These great regional city-states are ruled by lords who claim to be descended from the gods. This period of Maya success continues until AD900.

temple at Tikal

AD615 The great Maya leader Lord Pacal rules in the city of Palenque.

AD650 The city of Teotihuacan begins to decline. It is looted and burned by unknown invaders around AD700.

AD684 Lord Pacal's rule in Palenque ends. He is buried in a tomb within the Temple of the Inscriptions.

jade death mask of Lord Pacal

Bonampak mural

AD790 Splendid Maya wall-paintings are created in the royal palace in the city of Bonampak.

AD600   AD700   AD800

Between North and South

MESOAMERICA IS A LAND of contrasts. There are high, jagged mountains, harsh deserts and swampy lakes. In the north, volcanoes rumble. In the south, dense, steamy forests have constant rain for half the year. These features made travelling around difficult, and also restricted contact between the regions.

Mesoamerica was never ruled as a single, united country. For centuries it was divided into separate states, each based on a city that ruled the surrounding countryside. Different groups of people and their cities became rich and strong in turn, before their civilizations weakened and faded away.

Historians divide the Mesoamerican past into three main periods. In Preclassic times (2000BC–AD250), the Olmecs were most powerful. The Classic era (AD250–900) saw the rise of the Maya and the people living in the city of Teotihuacan. During the Postclassic era (AD900–1500), the Toltecs, followed by the Aztecs, controlled the strongest states.

Each civilization had its own language, laws, traditions and skills, but there were also many links between the separate states. They all built big cities and organized long-distance trade. They all practised human sacrifice and worshipped the same family of gods. And, unlike all other ancient American people, they all measured time using their own holy calendar of 260 days.

Sierra Madre Occidental

MEXICO

N

TIMELINE AD800–AD1400

AD800 The Maya palace-city of Palenque begins to decline.

AD856 The Toltecs of northern Mexico begin to create the city-state of Tula.

Palenque

AD900 Maya power begins to collapse. Many Maya cities, temples and palaces are deserted and overgrown by the rainforest. This is the beginning of the period known as the Postclassic era. The era lasts until AD1500.

AD950 The city of Tula becomes the centre of fast-growing Toltec power.

AD986 According to legend, the Toltec god-king Quetzalcoatl leaves north Mexico for the Maya lands of Yucatan.

Toltec warrior

AD1000 The Maya city of Chichen-Itza becomes powerful. Historians believe that the Maya may have been helped by Putun warriors from the Gulf coast of Mexico.

AD1000 Toltec merchants do business along long-distance trade routes around the coast. They are helped by Maya craftworkers. Long-distance trade has already been taking place in Mesoamerica for hundreds of years.

AD1011–1063 The Mixtecs are ruled by the leader Eight Deer, in the area of Oaxaca. The Mixtecs are master goldsmiths.

AD800   AD900   AD1000   AD110

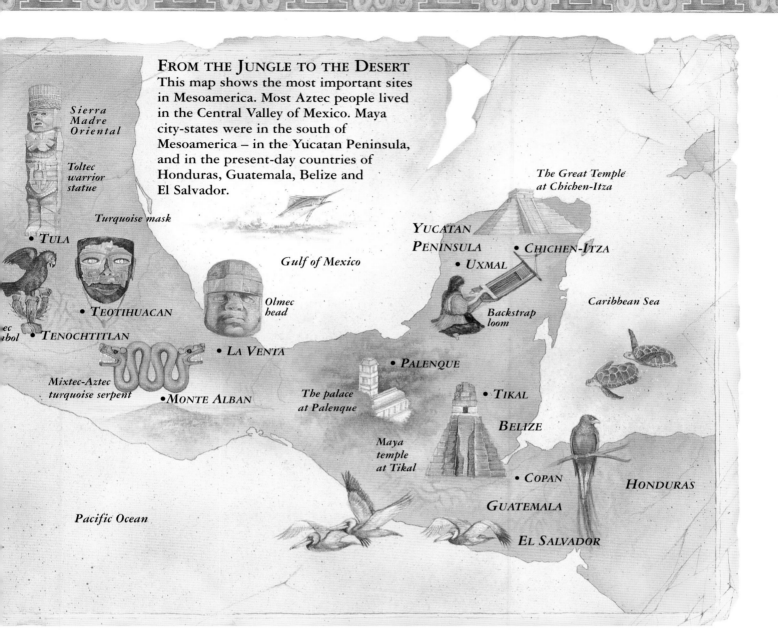

FROM THE JUNGLE TO THE DESERT

This map shows the most important sites in Mesoamerica. Most Aztec people lived in the Central Valley of Mexico. Maya city-states were in the south of Mesoamerica – in the Yucatan Peninsula, and in the present-day countries of Honduras, Guatemala, Belize and El Salvador.

Sierra Madre Oriental

Toltec warrior statue

Turquoise mask

• *Tula*

• *Teotihuacan*

• *Tenochtitlan*

ec
abol

Mixtec-Aztec turquoise serpent

• *Monte Alban*

• *La Venta*

Olmec head

Gulf of Mexico

The Great Temple at Chichen-Itza

Yucatan Peninsula

• *Chichen-Itza*

• *Uxmal*

Backstrap loom

Caribbean Sea

• *Palenque*

The palace at Palenque

• *Tikal*

Belize

Maya temple at Tikal

• *Copan*

Guatemala

El Salvador

Honduras

Pacific Ocean

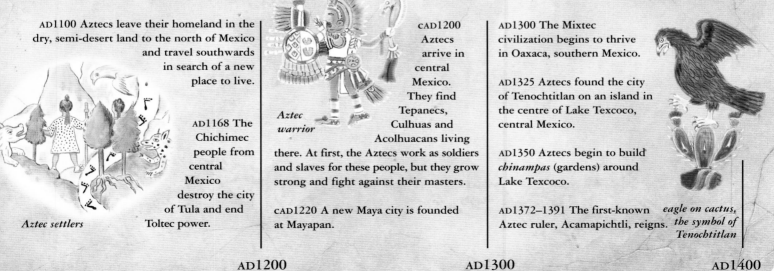

AD1100 Aztecs leave their homeland in the dry, semi-desert land to the north of Mexico and travel southwards in search of a new place to live.

AD1168 The Chichimec people from central Mexico destroy the city of Tula and end Toltec power.

Aztec settlers

Aztec warrior

CAD1200 Aztecs arrive in central Mexico. They find Tepanecs, Culhuas and Acolhuacans living there. At first, the Aztecs work as soldiers and slaves for these people, but they grow strong and fight against their masters.

CAD1220 A new Maya city is founded at Mayapan.

AD1300 The Mixtec civilization begins to thrive in Oaxaca, southern Mexico.

AD1325 Aztecs found the city of Tenochtitlan on an island in the centre of Lake Texcoco, central Mexico.

AD1350 Aztecs begin to build *chinampas* (gardens) around Lake Texcoco.

AD1372–1391 The first-known Aztec ruler, Acamapichtli, reigns.

eagle on cactus, the symbol of Tenochtitlan

AD1200

AD1300

AD1400

Famous People

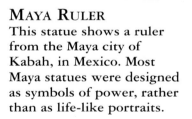

FAME IN Maya and Aztec times usually came with power. We know the names of powerful Aztec and Maya rulers, and sometimes of their wives. However, very few ordinary people's names have been discovered.

Rulers' names were written in a codex or carved on a monument to record success in battle or other great achievements. Scribes also compiled family histories, in which rulers often claimed to be descended from gods. This gave them extra religious power. Aztec and Maya rulers made sure their names lived on by building huge palaces, amazing temples and tombs.

Some of the most famous Mesoamerican rulers lived at a time when their civilization was under threat from outsiders. Explorers from Europe have left us detailed accounts and descriptions of the rulers they met.

ROYAL TOMB
This pyramid-shaped temple was built to house the tomb of Lord Pacal. He ruled the Maya city-state of Palenque from AD615 to 684. Its walls are decorated with scenes from Pacal's life.

MAYA RULER
This statue shows a ruler from the Maya city of Kabah, in Mexico. Most Maya statues were designed as symbols of power, rather than as life-like portraits.

TIMELINE AD1400–AD1600

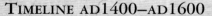

tribute items collected by the Aztecs

AD1400–AD1425 The Aztec city of Tenochtitlan continues to thrive and grow.

AD1415–1426 The Aztec leader Chimalpopoca reigns.

AD1428 Aztecs defeat the Tepanecs and begin to conquer neighbouring lands and collect tribute from them.

AD1428 Aztecs set up the Triple Alliance. This was an agreement with neighbouring city-states Texcoco and Tlacopan that made them the strongest force in Mexico.

AD1440 Moctezuma Ilhuicamina, the greatest Aztec ruler, begins his reign. He reigns until 1468.

AD1441 The Maya city of Mayapan is destroyed by civil war.

AD1468 Aztec ruler Axayacatl reigns.

AD1473 The Aztecs conquer the rich market-city of Tlatelolco in central Mexico.

market traders in the market-city of Tlatelolco

AD1400   AD1425   AD1450   AD147

GOLD-SEEKER

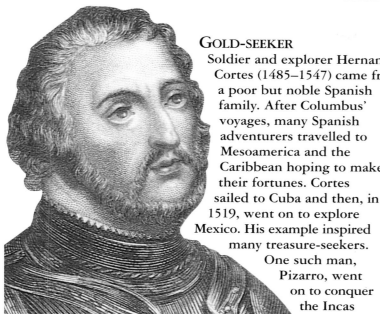

Soldier and explorer Hernan Cortes (1485–1547) came from a poor but noble Spanish family. After Columbus' voyages, many Spanish adventurers travelled to Mesoamerica and the Caribbean hoping to make their fortunes. Cortes sailed to Cuba and then, in 1519, went on to explore Mexico. His example inspired many treasure-seekers. One such man, Pizarro, went on to conquer the Incas of Peru.

THE LAST EMPEROR

Aztec emperor Moctezuma II (*above right*) ruled from 1502 to 1520. He was the last emperor to control the Aztec lands. Moctezuma II was a powerful warrior and a good administrator, but he was tormented by gloomy prophecies and visions of disaster. He was captured when Cortes and his soldiers invaded the capital city of Tenochtitlan in 1519. The following year he was stoned in a riot whilst trying to plead with his own people.

BETWEEN TWO WORLDS

Malintzin (*far right above*) was from a Mesoamerican state hostile to the Aztecs. She was of vital help to the Spanish conquerors because she spoke the Aztec language and quickly learned Spanish. The Spanish called her Doña Marina.

AD1481–1486 Aztec ruler Tizoc reigns.

AD1486 Aztec ruler Ahuitzotl begins his reign.

AD1487 The Aztecs' Great Temple in Tenochtitlan is finished. Twenty thousand captives are sacrificed at a special ceremony to consecrate it (make it holy).

AD1492 The European explorer Christopher Columbus sails across the Atlantic Ocean to America.

Columbus lands

AD1502 Columbus sails along the coast of Mesoamerica and meets Maya people.

a comet appears in the sky

AD1502–1520 Moctezuma II reigns. During his reign, a comet appears in the sky. Aztec astronomers fear that this, and other strange signs, mean the end of the world.

AD1519 Hernan Cortes, a Spanish soldier, arrives in Mexico. A year later, Cortes and his soldiers attack Tenochtitlan. Moctezuma II is killed.

AD1521 The Spanish destroy Tenochtitlan.

AD1525 Spain takes control of Aztec lands.

AD1527 Maya lands are invaded by the Spanish.

AD1535 Mexico becomes a Spanish colony.

AD1600 War and European diseases wipe out 10 million Aztecs, leaving fewer than a million, but the Aztec language and many customs live on. By AD1600, between 75% and 90% of Maya people are also dead, but Maya skills, beliefs and traditions survive.

Spanish soldier

AD1500   AD1525   AD1600

The Order of Things

MESOAMERICAN CITY-STATES were ruled by leaders with three separate tasks. They were army commanders, law-makers and priests. Many rulers claimed to be descended from the gods. Rulers were almost always men. Mesoamerican women – especially among the Maya – had important religious duties but rarely took part in law-making or army life.

Maya rulers were called *ahaw* (lord) or *mahk'ina* (great Sun lord), and each city-state had its own royal family. The Aztec leader was called the *tlatoani* (speaker). Originally, he was elected from army commanders by the Aztec people. Later, he was chosen from the family of the previous ruler. He ruled all Aztec lands, helped by a deputy called *cihuacoatl* (snake woman), by nobles and by army commanders. Priests observed the stars, looking for signs about the future, and held religious ceremonies.

Rulers, priests and nobles made up a tiny part of society. Ordinary citizens were called *macehualtin*. Women looked after their families. Men were farmers, fishermen or craftworkers. There were also thousands of slaves, who were criminals, enemy captives or poor people who had given up their freedom in return for food and shelter.

OFFICIAL HELP
This Maya clay figure shows a scribe at work. Well-trained officials, such as this scribe, helped Mesoamerican rulers by keeping careful records. Scribes also painted ceremonial pottery.

MAYA NOBLEWOMAN
This terracotta figure of a Maya noblewoman dates from between AD600 and 900. She is richly attired and is protecting her face with a parasol. Women did not usually hold official positions of responsibility in Mesoamerican lands. Instead queens and other noblewomen influenced their husbands by offering tactful suggestions and wise advice. Whether she was rich or poor, a woman's main duty was to provide children for her husband and to support him in all aspects of his work.

HONOUR TO THE KING
Painted pottery vases like this were buried alongside powerful Maya people. They show scenes from legends and royal palace life. Here, a lord presents tribute to the king.

THE RULING CLASS

A noble is shown getting ready for a ceremony in this Aztec codex picture. Aztec nobles played an important part in government. They were chosen by rulers to be judges, army commanders and officials. Nobles with government jobs paid no taxes and were given a free house to live in. Noblemen and women were born into ancient noble families, related to the rulers. It was, however, possible for an ordinary man to achieve higher rank if he fought very bravely in battle and captured four enemy soldiers alive.

MEN AT WORK

Here, Aztec farmers are harvesting ripe cobs of maize. This painting comes from the Florentine Codex. This 12-volume manuscript was made by a Spanish friar. Codex pictures like this tell us a lot about ordinary peoples' everyday lives. Notice how simply the farmers are dressed compared to the more powerful people on these pages.

WAR LEADER

This Maya stone carving shows ruler Shield Jaguar (*below left*) getting ready to lead his army in AD724. He is wearing a padded tunic and holding a knife in his right hand. His wife, Lady Xoc, is handing him his jaguar headdress. Maya rulers also took part in religious ceremonies, where they offered drops of their blood to the gods to ask for their help.

The Court, Government and Laws

THE REMAINS OF MANY splendid palaces survive in Mesoamerican lands. In the 1500s European explorers described the vast palace of the Aztec ruler Moctezuma II in Tenochtitlan. It had banqueting rooms big enough to seat 3,000 guests, private apartments, a library, a schoolroom, kitchens, stores, an arsenal for weapons, separate women's quarters, spectacular gardens and a large zoo. Etiquette around the emperor was very strict. Captains of the royal bodyguard had to approach Moctezuma barefoot, with downcast eyes, making low bows and murmuring, "Lord, my lord, my great lord." When they left, they had to walk backwards, keeping their gaze away from his face.

Palaces were not just rulers' homes. They were also official government headquarters where rulers greeted ambassadors from neighbouring city-states and talked with advisors.

Rulers also had the power to make strict laws. Each city-state had its own law-courts, where formidable judges had the power of life and death over people brought before them.

THE SEAT OF POWER
This carved jade ornament shows a seated Maya king. Although Aztec and Maya leaders had the final responsibility for decisions, they also relied on judges, officials and scribes to help them rule.

ROYAL RECORD
Maya rulers set up carved stone pillars in their cities to record major events during their reigns. These pillars are called stelae. This one celebrates a Maya ruler in Copan, Honduras.

MAKE A FEATHER FAN

You will need: pencil, thick card, scissors, thin red card, green paper, double-sided tape, feathers (real or paper), masking tape, paints, paintbrushes, coloured felt, PVA glue and brush, sticky tape, coloured wool, bamboo cane.

1 Draw two rings about 45cm in diameter and 8cm wide on thick card. Cut them out. Make another ring the same size from thin red card, as above.

2 Cut lots of leaf shapes from green paper. Stick them around the edge of one thick card ring using double-sided tape. Add some real or paper feathers.

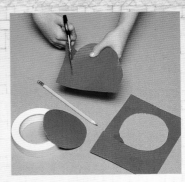

3 Cut two circles about 12cm in diameter from thin red card. Draw around something the right size, such as a reel of tape. These are for the centre of the fan.

LOCKED UP

Here, a group of Aztec judges discusses how to punish two prisoners. You can see them cowering in a wooden cage. By modern standards, punishments were very severe. If ordinary citizens broke the law, they might be beaten or speared with cactus spines. For a second offence, they might be stoned to death.

THE RULE OF THE GODS

This stone carving shows a human face being swallowed by a magic serpent. Royal and government buildings were often decorated with carvings such as this. They signified the religious power of the ruler of a particular city.

FIT FOR A KING

This picture from an Aztec codex shows visitors to a ruler's palace. It was reported by Spanish explorers that over six hundred nobles came to the Aztec ruler's palace every day to attend council meetings, consult palace officials, ask favours from the ruler and make their views heard. The ruler would sit on a mat on the floor with his council, as was the Aztec tradition.

Aztec nobles and rulers cooled themselves with beautiful feather fans.

4 Paint a flower on one of the two smaller red circles and a butterfly on the other. Cut v-shapes from the felt and glue them to the large red ring.

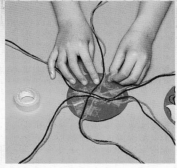

5 Using sticky tape, fix lengths of coloured wool to the back of one of the red circles, as shown. Place the red circle in the centre of the ring with leaves.

6 Tape the lengths of wool to the outer ring to look like spokes. Coat the ring with PVA glue and place the second card ring on top, putting a cane in between.

7 Use double-sided tape to stick the second red circle face up in the centre. Glue the red ring with felt v-shapes on top of the second thick card ring.

Family Life

FAMILIES WERE very important in Maya and Aztec times. By working together, family members provided themselves with food, jobs, companionship and a home. Each member of a family had special responsibilities. Men produced food or earned money to buy it. Women cared for babies and the home. From the age of about five or six, children were expected to do their share of the family's work by helping their parents. Because family life was so important, marriages were often arranged by a young couple's parents, or by a matchmaker. The role of matchmaker would be played by an old woman who knew both families well. Boys and girls got married when they were between 16 and 20 years old. The young couple usually lived in the boy's parents' home.

Aztec families belonged to local clan-groups, known as *calpulli*. Each *calpulli* chose its own leader, collected its own taxes and built its own temple. It offered help to needy families, but also kept a close eye on how members behaved. If someone broke the law, the whole clan might be punished for that person's actions.

MOTHER AND SON
These Maya clay figures may show a mother and her son. Boys from noble families went to school at about 15. They learned reading, writing, maths, astronomy and religion.

PAINFUL PUNISHMENT
This codex painting shows a father holding his son over a fire of burning chillies as a punishment. Aztec parents used severe punishments in an attempt to make their children honest and obedient members of society.

SPICE
Hot, spicy chilli peppers were an essential part of many Maya and Aztec meals. In fact, the Aztecs said that if a meal lacked chillies, it was a fast, not a feast! Chillies were used in stews and in spicy sauces, and they were used in medicine too. They were crushed and rubbed on aching muscles or mixed with salt to ease toothache.

red chillies

dried chillies, preserved for winter use

green chillies

IXTILTON

This Aztec mask is made of a black volcanic stone called obsidian. It shows the god Ixtilton, helper of Huitzilopochtli, the Aztecs' special tribal god. Aztec legends told how Ixtilton could bring darkness and peaceful sleep to tired children.

HUSBAND AND WIFE

The bride and groom in this codex picture of an Aztec wedding have their clothes tied together. This shows that their lives are now joined. Aztec weddings were celebrated with presents and feasting. Guests carried bunches of flowers, and the bride wore special make-up with her cheeks painted yellow or red. During the ceremony, the bride and groom sat side by side on a mat in front of the fire.

GUARDIAN GODDESS

The goddess Tlazolteotl is shown in this codex picture. She was the goddess of lust and sin. Tlazolteotl was also said to watch over mothers and young children. Childbirth was the most dangerous time in a woman's life, and women who died in childbirth were honoured like brave soldiers.

LEARNING FOR LIFE

A mother teaches her young daughter to cook in this picture from an Aztec codex. The girl is making tortillas, which are flat maize pancakes. You can see her grinding the corn in a *metate* (grinding stone) using a *mano* (stone used with the metate). Aztec mothers and fathers trained their children in all the skills they would need to survive in adult life. Children from the families of expert craftworkers learned their parents' special skills.

In the Home

MESOAMERICAN HOMES were not just safe places to eat and sleep. They were workplaces too. There were no refrigerators or household appliances, so women had to work hard preparing food for the day's meals or for winter storage. Vegetables were cleaned and chopped with stone knives, as there were no metal ones. Beans and chillies were spread out in the Sun to dry, and maize kernels were ground into flour. Homes had to be kept clean as well. Firewood and water had to be fetched and clothes washed. Women and girls spent long hours spinning thread and weaving it into cloth, then sewing it into tunics and cloaks for the family. Some women wove cloth to sell or to give to the government as a tax payment. Homes were also where most sick or elderly people were cared for.

HEART OF THE HOME
Throughout Mesoamerica, the hearth-fire was the heart of the home. This statue shows Xiuhtecuhtli, the Aztec god of fire. The top of his head is hollow, so a fire can be kindled there. The rays on his headdress represent flickering flames.

MAYA POT
The Maya decorated ceremonial pottery with pictures of gods, kings and important people. This pot shows a maize merchant. Pottery used in the home for food and drink would be less ornate.

A BACKSTRAP LOOM
You will need: paintbrush, water-based paint, 2 pieces of thick dowel about 70 cm long, string, scissors, thick card, masking tape, coloured wool.

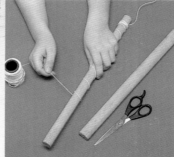

1 Paint the pieces of dowel brown. Leave them to dry. Tie string to each dowel and wind it around. Leave a length of string loose at each end.

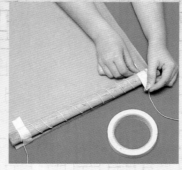

2 Cut a piece of thick card about 70cm x 100cm. This is a temporary base. Lightly fix the stringed dowels to it at the shorter sides with masking tape.

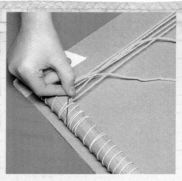

3 Now take your yellow wool. Thread the wool through the string loops and pull through to the other end, as shown. Try to keep the yellow wool taut.

GLOWING COLOURS

Many craftworkers worked at home. This painting by Diego Rivera shows craftworkers from the region of Tarascan dying hanks of yarn before they are woven into cloth. Mesoamerican dyes were made from fruits, flowers, shellfish and the cochineal beetles that lived on cactus plants. Only rich people were allowed to wear clothes made from brightly coloured cloth. Poorer people wore natural colours.

A HELPING HAND

Aztec girls were meant to make themselves useful by helping their mothers around the home. This Aztec codex picture shows a girl sweeping the floor with a bundle of twigs.

WEAVING

Threads spun from plant fibres were woven into cloth on backstrap looms. The finest fabric was made from silky cotton. Rough yucca and cactus fibres made a coarser cloth. Looms like this are still used in Mexico today.

To weave, take the loom off the cardboard. Tie the loose string around your waist. Attach the other end of the loom to a post or tree with the string. Lean back to keep the long warp threads evenly taut.

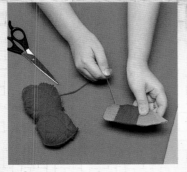

4 Cut a rectangle of thick card (300mm x 35mm). Now cut a small rectangle of card with one pointed end, as shown. Wind red wool around it.

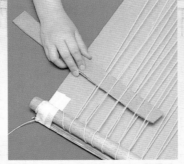

5 Now take your long card rectangle. This is your shed rod. Carefully slide it through every second thread on your loom, as shown.

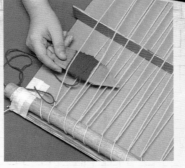

6 Turn your shed rod on its side. This will lift the threads up. Tie one end of your red wool to the yellow wool. Feed the card of wool through the lifted threads.

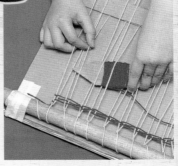

7 Lay the shed rod flat. Use the pointed end of your card to pick up each of the first or alternate threads. Thread the wool on the card through these.

Villages and Towns

MOST PEOPLE in Mesoamerica lived in country villages. They made a living from the land, taking their produce to nearby market towns to sell. Villages and towns all had to obey the strongest city in the region. Usually they also had to pay a tribute (a tax of goods or labour) to it as well. Villages were small, often with fewer than 50 families, but the biggest cities were huge. Historians estimate that over 150,000 people lived in the city of Teotihuacan in AD600. Cities, towns and villages were linked by roads cleared through the forest or by steep paths cut into mountain slopes.

The centre of most Mesoamerican cities was dedicated to religion. The greatest temples stood there, close to a vast open space used for holy ceremonies, dances and processions. Other important buildings, such as royal palaces and ball-courts, stood close by. The homes and workshops of ordinary citizens were built outside the ceremonial area.

HIDDEN IN THE TREES
Today the remains of the great Maya city of Tikal are almost hidden by the rainforest. In Maya times, the trees would have been felled to make room for houses and fields. In around AD800, about 50,000 people lived here.

DESERT FRUITS
Several kinds of cactus thrive in Mexico's dry, semi-desert, regions. The prickly pear had a sweet, juicy fruit, but the maguey cactus was even more useful. Its sap was used as a sweetener and to make an alcoholic drink. Its fibres were made into clothing and baskets. Its spines were used as needles.

BIG CITY
The Maya city of Copan in present-day Honduras covered an enormous area, perhaps 13km long and 3km wide. The religious centre and the nearby Great Plaza are shown here. Both were rebuilt in splendid style on the orders of King Yax Pac around AD750. The temples and royal palace are painted a glowing red – the colour of life and power.

quetzal

humming bird

parrot

BIRDS OF A FEATHER
These little pictures are from an Aztec codex. They show just some of the many beautiful wild birds that lived in Mesoamerica. The Maya and the Aztecs hunted many of them for their brightly coloured feathers. These feathers could then be used to make fans or shields.

toucan

parrot

MOUNTAINS AND MAIZE
On steep, cold mountain slopes, such as those of Popocatapetl, farmers grew hardy crops. *Chia* and *huautli* were both bushy plants with edible seeds. They were well suited to this environment. In sunny, fertile areas, maize was grown.

owl

crocodile

FROM DESERT TO RAINFOREST
The landscape of Mesoamerica is extremely varied. Many different creatures, from crocodiles to deer inhabit it. The Maya and the Aztecs hunted many of these animals for their meat or skins.

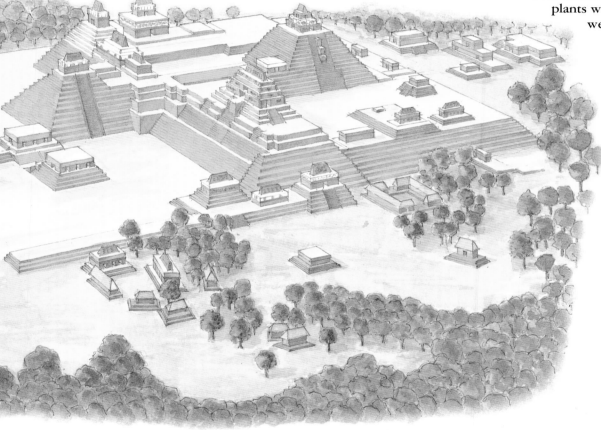

deer

butterfly

rabbit

snake

Buildings and Houses

PEOPLE LIVING in Mesoamerica used local materials for building. They had no wheeled transport, so carrying building materials long distances was quite difficult. Stone was the most expensive and longest-lasting building material. It was used for religious buildings, rulers' palaces and tombs. The homes of ordinary people were built more quickly and easily of cheaper materials, such as Sun-dried mud bricks, called adobe, or mud smeared over a framework of wooden poles. For strength, the walls might have stone foundations.

All Mesoamerican homes were very simply furnished. There were no chairs or tables, curtains or carpets — just some jars and baskets for storage and a few reed mats. Everyone, from rulers to slaves, sat and slept on mats on the floor. Most ordinary Aztec homes were L-shaped or built around a courtyard, with a separate bathroom for washing and a small shrine to the gods in the main room.

FAMILY HOME
This present-day Maya family home is built in traditional style, with red-painted mud-and-timber walls. It has one door and no windows. The floor is made of pounded earth. The roof, thatched with dried grass, is steeply sloped so the rain runs off it.

BURIED UNDERGROUND
Archaeologists have discovered these remains of houses at the Maya city of Copan. The roofs, walls and doors have rotted away, but we can still see the stone foundations. The houses are small and tightly packed together.

MAKE A MAYA HOUSE

You will need: thick card, pencil, ruler, scissors, glue, masking tape, terracotta plaster paste (or thin plaster coloured with paint), balsa wood strips, water pot, wide gummed paper tape, brush, short lengths of straw.

Back wall 20cm × 12cm

Side wall 10cm × 12cm

Side wall with fence 16cm × 12cm (10cm top)

Front of house 12cm (8cm, 6cm, 6cm)

Roof x 2 (18cm top, 23cm bottom, 10cm)

Side of roof x 2 (10 cm, 13cm)

Draw the shapes of the roof and walls of the house on to thick card, using the measurements shown. (Please note that the templates are not shown to scale.) Cut the pieces out.

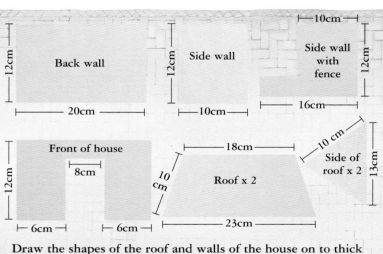

1 Cut out a rectangle 25cm x 15cm from thick card for the base. Stick the house walls and base together with glue. Use masking tape for support.

STONEMASONS AT WORK

Mesoamerican masons constructed massive buildings using very simple equipment. Their wedges were made from wood, and their mallets and hammers were shaped from hard volcanic stone. Until around AD900 metal tools were unknown. Fine details were added by polishing stonework with wet sand.

PLASTER

Big stone buildings, such as temples, were often covered with a kind of plaster called stucco. This was then painted with ornate designs. Plaster was made by burning limestone and mixing it with water and coloured earth. By the 1400s, there was so much new building in Tenochtitlan that the surrounding lake became polluted with chemicals from the plaster making.

plaster

limestone

SKILFUL STONEWORK

This carved stone panel from the Maya city of Chichen-Itza is decorated with a pattern of crosses. It was used to provide a fine facing to thick walls made of rubble and rough stone. This wall decorates a palace building.

A Maya house provided a cool shelter from the very hot Mexican Sun, as well as keeping out rain.

2 Paint the walls and base with plaster paste. This will make them look like Sun-dried mud. You could also decorate the doorway with balsa wood strips.

3 Put the house on one side to dry. Take your roof pieces and stick them together with glue. Use masking tape to support the roof, as shown.

4 Moisten the wide paper tape and use it to cover the joins between the roof pieces. There should be no gaps. Then cover the whole roof with glue.

5 Press lengths of straw into the glue on the roof. Work in layers, starting at the bottom. Overlap the layers. Fix the roof to the house using glue.

Farming

PEOPLE LIVING in different regions of Mesoamerica used various methods to cultivate their land. Farmers in the rainforests grew maize, beans and pumpkins in fields they cleared by slashing and burning. They cut down thick, tangled bushes and vines, leaving the tallest trees standing. Then they burned all the chopped-down bushes and planted seeds in the ashes. But the soil was only fertile for a few years. The fields were left to turn back into forest, and new ones were cleared. Maya farmers also grew crops in raised fields. These were plots of land along the edge of rivers and streams, heaped up with rich, fertile silt dug from the riverbed.

Aztec farmers planted maize wherever they could, on steep rocky hillsides and the flat valley floor. But they grew their biggest crops of fruit, flowers and vegetables in gardens called *chinampas*. These were reclaimed from the marshy shallows along the shores of Lake Texcoco and around the island city of Tenochtitlan.

MAIZE GOD
This stone statue shows Yum Caax (Lord of the Forest Bushes), the Maya god of maize. It was found at Copan. All Mesoamerican people honoured maize goddesses or gods, as the crop was so important.

DIGGING STICKS
Mesoamerican farmers had no tractors, horses or heavy ploughs to help them prepare their fields. Instead, a sharp-bladed wooden digging stick, called an *uictli*, was used for planting seeds and hoeing weeds. Some farmers in Mesoamerica today find digging sticks are more efficient than the kind of spade traditionally used in Europe.

FIELD WORK
This painting by Mexican artist Diego Rivera shows Aztecs using digging sticks to hoe fields of maize. You can see how dry the soil is. If the May rains failed, or frosts came early, a whole year's crop would be lost. Mesoamerican farmers made offerings to the rain god between March and October.

Chinampa soil was made even more fertile by using human manure.

Sticky mud was collected from the lake bottom. Along with compost and manure, this mud was poured on top of the chinampas.

The chinampa was held together by stakes, thick water vegetation and the tangled roots of trees.

FLOATING GARDENS

Chinampas were a sort of floating garden. They were made by sinking layers of twigs and branches under the surface of the lake and weighting them with stones. *Chinampas* were so productive that the government passed laws telling farmers when to sow seeds. This ensured there would be a steady supply of vegetables and flowers for sale in the market.

SLASH AND BURN

Mesoamerican farmers used a technique called slash and burn to clear land for farming. Crops grew very quickly in Mesoamerica's warm climate.

VEGETARIANS

Many ordinary Mesoamerican people survived on a largely vegetarian diet, based on maize and beans. This would be supplemented by other fresh fruits and vegetables in season. Meat and fish were expensive, luxury foods. Only rulers and nobles could afford to eat them every day.

beans

prickly pear

FOREST FRUITS

This Aztec codex painting shows men and women gathering cocoa pods from trees. Cocoa was so valuable that it was sent as tribute to Tenochtitlan.

Hunting and Gathering

MESOAMERICAN FARMERS did not rear many animals to kill for food. Before the Spaniards arrived, there were no cows, sheep, pigs or horses in their lands. Most meat and fish came from wild creatures, which were hunted or trapped. Deer, hares, rabbits and foxes were hunted on the dry mountain slopes. Peccary (wild boar), armadillos and opossums sheltered in the forests. Aztec hunters trapped ducks, geese and pelicans in shallow reed-beds beside the lake. Maya fishermen caught turtles, dolphins and shellfish all around the coast.

Hunters also went in search of many wild creatures that were not used for food. Millions of brightly-coloured birds were killed for their feathers. Poisonous snakes and fierce pumas, jaguars and ocelots (wild cats) were hunted for their beautiful furs and skins.

Mesoamerican people also gathered a great many plants and insects for other uses. Seeds, leaves, bark and flowers were used for medicine and to make paper, mats and baskets. Wild bees supplied honey, and locusts were eaten as snacks.

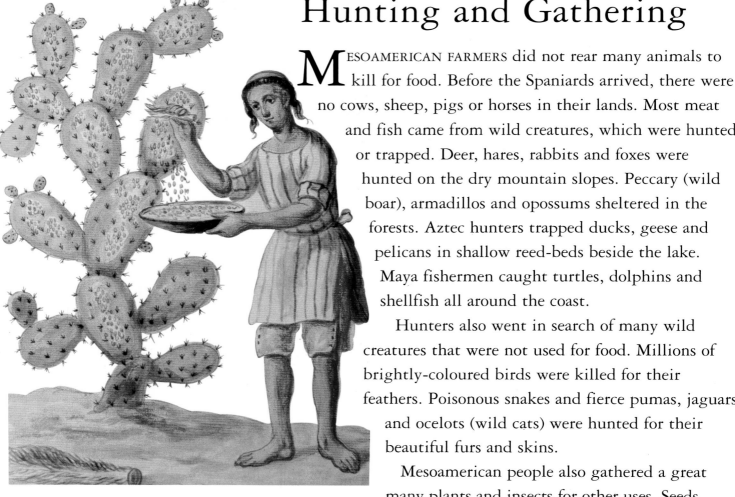

INSECT HARVEST
Mesoamerican people collected many kinds of insects for use in medicines, as dyes and as food. This codex picture shows cochineal beetles being gathered from a cactus. It took about 70,000 beetles to make half a kilo of red dye.

HUNTERS
Mesoamerican men went hunting with bows and arrows, slings, clubs and spears. Hunters' bows were made of wood, and their arrows were tipped with obsidian, a sharp volcanic glass. Their clubs were made from lumps of rock lashed to wooden handles with rope or leather thongs. To make their spears fly further, they used an *atlatl*. This was a grooved piece of wood that acted like an extra-long arm to increase the power behind the throw.

CHOCOLATE TREE

This picture from an Aztec codex shows a cocoa tree and two Aztec gods. Cocoa pods could be gathered from cocoa trees all over Mesoamerica. Once ground, the cocoa beans were mixed with water to make chocolate. Chocolate was a highly prized drink and only nobles could afford to drink it. It was often sweetened with honey and flavoured with vanilla. The Aztecs and Maya did not know how to make bars of solid chocolate, like those we enjoy today.

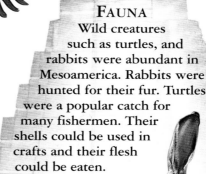

FAUNA

Wild creatures such as turtles, and rabbits were abundant in Mesoamerica. Rabbits were hunted for their fur. Turtles were a popular catch for many fishermen. Their shells could be used in crafts and their flesh could be eaten.

turtle   *blacktail jackrabbit*

FEATHER TRADE

Mesoamerican merchants brought feathers from hunters who lived in the rainforest. The picture above shows different kinds of feathers sorted and ready for sale.

SEA PRODUCE

This Maya beaker is decorated with a picture of a god emerging from a shell. Beautiful seashells were highly prized in Mesoamerica and were often used in jewellery and craftwork. One species of shellfish was caught for its sticky slime. This slime was milked from the shellfish and then used to make a rich purple dye.

fishermen used sticks and paddles to drive fish into nets

flat-bottomed boats could sail across Mexico's shallow, marshy lakes

RIVERS AND LAKES

In this Aztec codex picture, we can see a boy fishing. He is standing in a flat-bottomed boat, hollowed from a single log. This boy is using a bag-shaped net, woven from cactus fibre. Fish were also caught with hooks, lines and harpoons. Long nets, draped across canoes, were used to catch waterfowl.

Food and Drink

MESOAMERICAN PEOPLE usually had two meals a day. They ate their main meal around noon and a smaller snack in the evening. Ordinary people's food was plain and simple but very healthy – if they could get enough of it. When crops failed, there was famine. Everyday meals were based on maize, beans, vegetables and fruit. Peppers, tomatoes, pumpkins and avocado pears were popular vegetables, but the Aztecs also ate boiled cactus leaves (with the spines removed!). Gruel made from wild sage or amaranth seeds was also a favourite. Meat and fish were luxuries. Deer, rabbit, turkey and dog were cooked for feasts, along with frogs, lizards and turtles. The Aztecs also ate fish eggs and green algae from the lake.

USEFUL POTS

Mesoamerican people did not have metal cooking pots, so women cooked and served food in pottery bowls. Special pottery dishes were also used for specific jobs, such as cooking tortillas. The ones above were used for grating chillies and sweet peppers. They have rough ridged bases.

CACTUS WINE

Sweet, sticky sap from the maguey cactus was collected in leather flasks, then left to ferment in open troughs. It quickly turned into a strong alcoholic wine, which the Aztecs called *pulque*. Aztec men and women were not usually allowed to drink much alcohol. On special festivals honouring the dead, *pulque* was served by women wine-makers from huge pottery jars.

MAKE TORTILLAS

You will need: scales, 225g plain or maize flour, 1 tsp salt, bowl, 40g butter, jug, 120ml cold water, spoon, a little plain flour for kneading and flouring, rolling pin, pastry board, butter or oil for frying, frying pan.

1 Carefully weigh out the ingredients. If you cannot find maize flour, use plain flour instead. Aztec cooks had to grind their own flour.

2 Mix the flour and salt together in a bowl. Rub the butter into the mixture with your fingers until it looks like breadcrumbs. Then pour in the water.

3 Use your hands to mix everything together until you have a loose ball of dough. Do not worry if there is still some dry mixture around the bowl.

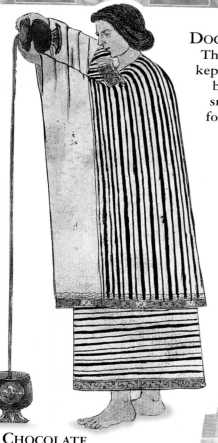

DOG FOOD
The Aztecs kept several breeds of small dog for eating.

TORTILLAS AND TAMALES
This painting shows women grinding maize kernels into flour on a flat stone. They then shaped balls of raw dough into pancakes (tortillas) and stuffed dumplings (tamales). Tortillas were cooked on a hot baking-stone, while tamales were baked in a shallow dish.

CHOCOLATE
Maya cooks dried and pounded cocoa pod seeds into a thick paste. This was then boiled with water. To make the mixture smooth and frothy, they poured it from one bowl to another, often from a great height.

NEW FOOD
In the years after the conquest of Mesoamerica, many vegetables were introduced to Europe, Asia and the Middle East. At first, gardeners found them difficult to grow, and cooks did not know how to prepare them. But today, many meals include tomatoes, peppers, chillies and avocado pears.

tomato

avocado pear

You could eat your tortillas with spicy bean stew and juicy tomatoes, just like the Aztecs did.

4 Knead the dough for at least 10 minutes until it is smooth. If the dough or your hands get too sticky, add a little plain flour to the bowl.

5 Tip the dough out of the bowl on to a floured pastry board. Divide it into egg-sized balls, using your hands or a knife. You should have about 12 balls.

6 Sprinkle the board and the rolling pin with a little plain flour to stop the dough sticking. Then roll each ball of dough into a thin pancake shape.

7 Ask an adult to help you fry the tortillas, using a non-stick frying pan. Fry each tortilla for one minute per side. Use a little oil in the pan if you wish.

Keeping Healthy and Clean

MESOAMERICAN PEOPLE liked to keep themselves and their houses clean. They washed in river water, took sweat-baths and swept their rooms with brushes of twigs and leaves. However, despite their attempts to stay clean and healthy, illness was common. Diseases recorded in Aztec lands, for example, include dysentery, chest infections and skin complaints. Throughout Mesoamerica, children often died from infections or in accidents around the home. Women died in childbirth, and many men were killed in battle. People were considered old by the time they were 40. Aztec medicine was a mixture of herbalism, religion, magic and first aid. Aztec doctors gave out powerful herbal medicines and encouraged patients to say prayers and make offerings to the gods. Sometimes their cures worked, but often the patients died.

DOCTOR ON CALL
A woman and child are shown consulting a doctor in the local market in this picture by Diego Rivera. The Aztecs made medicines out of many different fruits and herbs, some of which could kill or seriously damage the patient.

FOREIGN BODIES
Spanish settlers brought deadly diseases, such as measles and smallpox, to the Aztec and Maya lands in Mesoamerica after the conquest. Because of this the population of central Mexico fell from around 12 million in 1519 to only one million in 1600.

BURNING REMEDY
This scene from an Aztec codex advises people how to deal with fleas on their body. Pine resin was applied to the affected area and set alight. Patients could drink only cold water.

RASH MOMENT
A woman is shown treating an outbreak of sores on this man's skin. The patient would then drink and bathe in cactus sap.

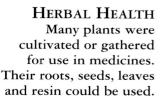

HERBAL HEALTH
Many plants were cultivated or gathered for use in medicines. Their roots, seeds, leaves and resin could be used.

DEADLY BITES
Many dangerous creatures lived in the deserts and rainforests of Mesoamerica. Bites from dangerous spiders and venomous snakes were common hazards. Herbal remedies, such as the roots of a tree called rabbit fern, were used to treat bites and stings.

tarantula　　　　*rattlesnake*

BROKEN SKULL
This man is suffering from a broken skull. The wound would be washed with urine to disinfect it.

BREAK A LEG
To cure broken limbs, the Aztecs would grind various roots into a powder. These were placed on the break. A splint would then be tied to the broken limb.

AFTER CARE
The man shown here is recovering from a broken leg. After 20 days, a poultice of lime and powdered cactus root would be applied to his leg. When the leg was strong, the patient was advised to take a hot bath.

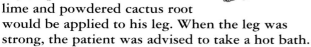

COUGH MIXTURE
A persistent cough could be cured by an infusion of *teouaxin* cooked with chilli and salt.

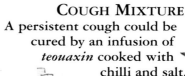

BATHING ILLNESS AWAY
Steam baths like this were used for keeping clean. The Aztecs also used them to try to cure illness. They believed the baths would drive out the evil spirits that caused many diseases. Steam baths worked like a present-day sauna. Bathers sat in a small cabin, close to a fire, which heated large stones. When the stones were very hot, water was poured over them, creating clouds of steam.

Clothes, Hairstyles, Jewellery

AZTEC CLOTHES were very simple. Women wore a skirt and tunic, while men had a cloak and loincloth. But clothes still revealed a lot about the wearer. Strict laws described suitable clothing for different people. Ordinary families were meant to wear plain, knee-length clothes woven from rough *ixtle* (cactus fibre) and no jewellery. Nobles were allowed to wear longer-length clothes of fine white cotton, decorated with embroidery or woven patterns. They could also wear earrings, necklaces, labrets (lip-plugs) and bracelets of gold and precious stones. Maya clothes were also simple – just strips of fabric wound around the body. Maya ideas of beauty would be strange to us. They filed their teeth and encouraged their children to grow up cross-eyed. Mothers also bound their babies' heads to flatten them.

GLITTERING GOLD
This gold chest ornament is in the shape of a skeleton-faced god. It was made by Mixtec goldsmiths from southern Mexico. Jewellery was worn only by nobles. In Mesoamerica, both noblemen and women wore fine jewellery.

CEREMONIAL CLOTHES
Musicians and actors walk in procession in this picture. It is copied from a wall painting in a Maya ruler's palace at Bonampak. The procession forms part of a celebration to honour the ruler's child. The men on the right are wearing white cloth headdresses and wrap-around skirts, tied with sashes at the waist.

MAKE A BAT BROOCH

You will need: pencil, thin card, scissors, black and gold paint, small paintbrush, paint pot, palette, glue, glue brush, string, small safety pin, masking tape.

1 Draw the shape of your brooch in pencil on thin card (6cm x 10cm). This brooch is based on a gold Aztec pendant shaped like a vampire bat god.

2 Carefully cut out the finished shape with scissors. Aztec jewellery designs were very delicate and complicated. They often featured gods.

3 Use black paint to colour in the eyes, mouth and hair of your bat, as shown above. It is best to use the paint fairly thickly.

CLOAK AND DAGGER

This Aztec warrior is wearing a long, brightly coloured cloak and an elaborate feather headdress. Aztec cloaks were simple rectangles of cloth, fastened at the shoulder by a knot. There were strict rules governing their length. Only nobles or soldiers who had legs that had been badly scarred in battle could wear cloaks like this one, coming below the knee. Ordinary men had to wear short cloaks.

MEXICAN STYLE

A Huastec woman from Veracruz, on the north coast of Mexico, is shown in this statue. She is wearing a wide tunic and a long skirt. Her hair is tied up in a carefully-folded headdress, and she wears a necklace and disc-shaped earrings. Although different patterns were favoured by the peoples of the various Mesoamerican cultures, the style of clothing was essentially very similar.

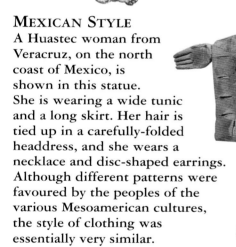

SKIRTS, TUNICS AND CLOAKS

A well-off Aztec couple sit by the fire, while their hostess cooks a meal. Both women are wearing long skirts. The bright embroidery of their tunics is a sign of high rank. Their long hair is braided and tied on top of their heads to make horns in a typical married woman's style. Girls and unmarried women wore their hair loose down their backs.

4 Cut teeth out of card and glue in place. Use the glue to stick string on the bat's face, head and body. Coil the string into spirals for the hair. Leave to dry.

5 Carefully paint the brooch all over (except for the black areas) with gold paint. Leave in a warm place for the paint to dry.

6 When the paint is dry, turn the brooch over and fix a safety pin on to the back with masking tape. Make sure it is secure.

You could wear your brooch on your chest, as the Aztecs did, or pin it on your sleeve.

Craftworkers

SPANISH EXPLORERS arriving in Mesoamerica were amazed at the wonderful objects they found there. They were better than anything they had seen in Europe. Pottery, jewellery, fabrics, mosaics, masks, knives and feather work were all made by skilled Mesoamerican craftworkers using simple, hand-powered tools. In big cities such as Tenochtitlan, Aztec craftworkers organized themselves into guilds. These made sure that all members worked to the highest standards and trained new workers. Many craft skills were passed from parents to children. Sometimes whole families worked as a team in workshops next to the family home.

MOSAIC MASK
This ritual mask is inlaid with a mosaic of turquoise. This valuable stone was brought back from mines in North America by Aztec traders.

Many Mesoamerican craft goods were decorated with beautiful patterns. Often, they had special religious meanings. Aztec warriors marched into battle carrying magic feathered shields. Jewellery was decorated with death's-head designs. Many Maya rulers and nobles were buried with elaborately decorated pots.

LIVING JEWELS
Featherworkers wove or glued thousands of feathers together to make headdresses, cloaks, warriors' uniforms, shields and fans. Men drew the designs on stiffened cloth and made light wooden frames to support the finished item. Women cleaned and sorted the feathers.

MAKE A MOSAIC MASK

You will need: balloon, petroleum jelly, newspaper, papier-mâché mixture (1 part PVA glue to 3 parts water), bowl, paintbrush, scissors, gummed paper tape, palette of paints, water pot, self-drying clay, card, plaster coloured with paint.

1 Inflate a balloon to the size of your head. Cover with petroleum jelly. Soak strips of newspaper in papier-mâché mixture. Add five layers to the front of the balloon.

2 Once dry, pop the balloon. Draw a mask shape on to the papier-mâché and cut it out. Use clay to add eyes and a nose. Cover the edges with gummed paper. Leave to dry.

3 Mix white and blue paint together to create three different shades. Paint one sheet of card with each. When dry, cut them into little pieces.

WARRIOR DISH
This dish was made in the Maya city of Tikal, in present-day Guatemala. It is painted with slip (a liquid clay coloured with minerals) and shows the figure of a warrior. All Mesoamerican pots were shaped by hand – the use of a potter's wheel was not known.

WOVEN TRIBUTE
Cloaks and blankets were sent as tribute to the great city of Tenochtitlan, as well as being sold in markets.

MOULDING GOLD
This painting by Diego Rivera shows Aztec goldsmiths with molten gold. Most jewellery was made by melting gold-dust in a furnace, then pouring it into a mould.

TREASURES
Mesoamerican people treasured many beautiful semi-precious stones, such as turquoise, obsidian and rock-crystal. They paid high prices for corals, pearls and shells from the sea. But they valued jade, a hard, smooth, deep-green stone, most of all, because it symbolized eternal life.

turquoise

obsidian

Aztec craftworkers carefully cut semi-precious stones into tiny squares. Turquoise, jade, shell and obsidian were all used for this purpose. The craftworkers used these pieces to create beautiful mosaic masks like this.

4 Cover the mask (except the eyes and mouth) with plaster paste. Press the card pieces into this, using glue to help any awkward ones to stick.

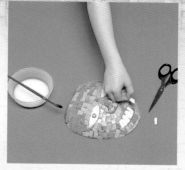

5 Paint the eyes with black and white paint. Cut out teeth from white card and carefully glue in position. Leave the mask in a warm place to dry.

6 Now coat the whole mask with a thin coat of PVA glue. This will seal the surface of the mask.

Merchants and Markets

THE MARKET PLACE was the heart of many Mesoamerican cities and towns. Traders, craftworkers and farmers met there to exchange their produce. Many market traders were women. They sold cloth or cooking pots, made by themselves or their families, and maize, fruit, flowers and vegetables grown by their husbands. In big cities, such as the trading centre of Tlatelolco, government officials also sold exotic goods that had been sent to the Aztec rulers as tribute (taxes) by conquered city-states. After the Aztecs conquered Tlatelolco in 1473, it soon became the greatest market in Mesoamerica. It was reported that almost 50,000 people came there on the busiest days.

Long-distance trade was carried out by merchants called *pochteca*. Gangs of porters carried their goods. The work was often dangerous, but the rewards were great.

MERCHANT GOD
Yacatecuhtli was the Aztec god of merchants and traders. In the codex picture above, he is shown standing in front of a crossroads marked with footprints. Behind him (*right*), is a tired porter with a load of birds on his back.

MAIZE MARKET
Mesoamerican farmers grew many different varieties of maize, with cobs that were pale cream, bright yellow, or even deep blue. Their wives took the maize to market, as selling was women's work. This modern wall-painting shows Aztec women buying and selling maize in the great market at Tlatelolco. At the market, judges sat in raised booths, keeping a lookout for thieves and cheats.

MAKE A MAYA POT
You will need: self-drying clay, board, rolling pin, masking tape, modelling tool, water bowl, small bowl, petroleum jelly, PVA glue, glue brush, yellow and black paint, paintbrush, water pot.

1 Roll out the clay until it is approximately 5mm thick. Cut out a base for the pot with a modelling tool. Use a roll of masking tape as a guide for size.

2 Roll out some long sausages of clay. Coil them around the base of the pot to build up the sides. Join and smooth the clay with water as you go.

3 Model a lip at the top of the pot. Leave it to dry. Cover a small bowl with petroleum jelly. Make a lid by rolling out some clay. Place the clay over the bowl.

JOURNEY'S END

This modern painting shows merchants and porters arriving at the market city of Tlatelolco. Such travellers made long journeys to bring back valuable goods, such as shells, jade and fig-bark paper. Young men joining the merchants' guild were warned about tiredness, pain and ambushes on their travels.

SKINS

Items such as puma, ocelot and jaguar skins could fetch a high price at market.

BARTER

Mesoamerican people did not have coins. They bought and sold by bartering, exchanging the goods they wanted to sell for other peoples' goods of equal value. Costly items such as gold-dust, quetzal feathers and cocoa beans were exchanged for goods they wanted to buy.

colourful feathers   *cocoa beans*

MARKET PRODUCE

In Mexico today, many markets are still held on the same sites as ancient ones. Many of the same types of foodstuffs are on sale there. In this modern photograph, we see tomatoes, avocados and vegetables that were also grown in Aztec times. Today, as in the past, most market traders and shoppers are women.

Mesoamerican potters made their pots by these coil or slab techniques. The potter's wheel was not used at all in Mesoamerica. The pots were sold at the local market.

4 Turn your pot upside down and place it over the rolled-out clay. Trim away the excess clay with a modelling tool by cutting around the top of the pot.

5 Use balls of clay to make a turtle to go on top of the lid. When both the lid and turtle are dry, use PVA glue to stick the turtle on to the centre of the lid.

6 Roll three small balls of clay of exactly the same size for the pot's feet. When they are dry, glue them to the base of the pot. Make sure they are evenly spaced.

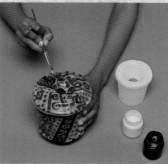
7 Paint the pot with Aztec designs in black and yellow. When you have finished, varnish the pot with a thin coat of PVA glue to make it shiny.

Travel and Transport

M ESOAMERICAN PEOPLE knew about wheels but they did not make wheeled transport of any kind. Carriages and carts would not have been suitable for journeys through dense rainforests or along steep, narrow mountain tracks. Many Maya cities were also linked by raised causeways that would have been difficult for wheeled vehicles to travel along.

Most people travelled overland on foot, carrying goods on their backs. Mesoamerican porters carried heavy loads with the help of a *tumpline*. This was a broad band of cloth that went across their foreheads and under the bundles on their backs, leaving their arms free. Rulers and nobles were carried in beds, called litters. On rivers and lakes, Mesoamericans used simple dug-out boats. At sea, Maya sailors travelled in huge wooden canoes that were able to make voyages of many kilometres in rough seas.

CARRIED HIGH
A Maya nobleman is shown being carried in a litter (portable bed) made from jaguar skins. Spanish travellers reported that the Aztec emperor was carried in the same way. Blankets were also spread in front of the emperor as he walked, to stop his feet touching the ground.

MEN OR MONSTERS?
Until the Spaniards arrived with horses in 1519, there were no animals big and strong enough to ride in the Mesoamerican lands. There were horses in America in prehistoric times, but they died out around 10,000BC. When the Aztecs saw the Spanish riding, they thought they were monsters – half man, half beast.

A WHEELED DOG

You will need: board, self-drying clay, 4 lengths of thin dowel about 5cm long and 2 lengths about 7cm long, water bowl, modelling tool, thick card, scissors, PVA glue, glue brush, paintbrush, modelling tool, paintbrush, paint, masking tape.

1 Roll a large piece of clay into a fat sausage to form the dog's body. Push the 5cm pieces of dowel into the body to make the legs. Leave to dry.

2 Cover the dowel legs with clay, extending the clay 2cm beyond the end of the dowel. Make a hole at the end of each leg with a piece of dowel. Leave to dry.

3 Push the dowel through the holes in the legs to join them horizontally. Make the dog's head and ears from clay. Join them to the body using water.

HARDWORKING PORTERS

This engraving from the 1900s shows Aztec slaves and commoners carrying loads for Spanish conquerors. Being a porter was very hard work. They were expected to cover up to 100 km per day, carrying about 25–30kg on their backs. Like most Mesoamerican people, they travelled these long distances barefoot.

BY BOAT

Aztec soldiers and the citizens of Tenochtitlan used boats with flat bottoms to travel around the city. Boats like this were also used to carry fruits and vegetables to market. Dug-out canoes were popular too. They were made from hollowed out tree trunks.

AZTEC WATERWAYS

The Aztecs paddled their canoes and flat-bottomed boats on Lake Texcoco. Today most of this lake has dried up. The lakeside *chinampas*, where they grew food and flowers, have almost disappeared. This photograph shows modern punts sailing along one of the last remaining Aztec waterways between the few *chinampas* that survive.

Toys like this dog are proof that the wheel was known in Mesoamerica. Wheeled vehicles were not suitable for rugged Mesoamerican land.

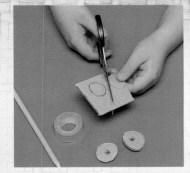

4 Cut four circles 3.5cm in diameter from card to make wheels. Pierce a hole in the centre of each. Make the holes big enough for the dowel to fit through.

5 Make four wheels from clay, the same size as the card wheels. Glue the clay and card wheels together. Make holes through the clay wheels and leave to dry.

6 Paint the dog's head, body, legs and wheels with Aztec patterns. When the paint is dry, give the dog a thin coat of PVA glue to act as a varnish.

7 Fit the wheels on to the ends of the dowels that pass through the dog's legs. Wrap strips of masking tape around the ends to stop the wheels falling off.

Warriors and Weapons

AZTEC ARMIES were very large. All Aztec men learned how to fight and had to be ready to hurry off to battle when they heard the sound of the great war drum outside the ruler's palace in Tenochtitlan. Ordinary soldiers wore tunics and leg-guards of padded cotton that had been soaked in saltwater. This made it tough – strong enough to protect the wearer from many fierce blows. Aztec army commanders wore splendid uniforms decorated with gold, silver, feathers and fur.

Both the Maya and the Aztecs greatly admired bravery. Aztec armies were led by nobles who had won promotion for brave deeds in battle, or for taking lots of captives. It was a disgrace for an Aztec soldier to try to save his own skin. It was more honourable for him to be killed fighting, or to be sacrificed, than to survive.

Maya soldiers went to war to win captives for sacrifice, but they also fought battles to control trade routes, to obtain tribute and to gain power. They wore a variety of garments, including sleeveless tunics, loincloths, fur costumes and cotton armour.

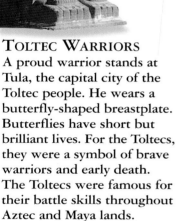

TOLTEC WARRIORS
A proud warrior stands at Tula, the capital city of the Toltec people. He wears a butterfly-shaped breastplate. Butterflies have short but brilliant lives. For the Toltecs, they were a symbol of brave warriors and early death. The Toltecs were famous for their battle skills throughout Aztec and Maya lands.

HELD CAPTIVE
An Aztec warrior is shown capturing an enemy in battle in this codex picture. The warrior is dragging his captive along by the hair. Young Aztec men had to grow their hair long at the back and could only cut it when they had taken their first prisoner in battle.

AN EAGLE HELMET

You will need: ruler, thick card, pencil, scissors, masking tape, stapler, self-drying clay, PVA glue, glue brush, gummed paper tape, paints, paintbrush, water pot, ribbon, felt, green paper, Velcro.

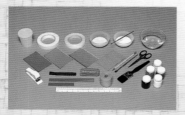

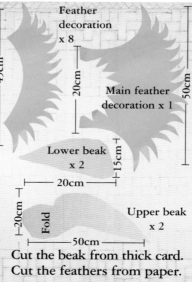

Feather decoration x 8

45cm

20cm

50cm

Main feather decoration x 1

Lower beak x 2

15cm

20cm

Upper beak x 2

20cm

Fold

50cm

Cut the beak from thick card. Cut the feathers from paper.

1 Make your helmet by joining the two parts of the upper beak with masking tape. Join the two parts of the lower beak in the same way, as shown.

2 Fold the two rounded ends of the upper beak towards each other and staple them together. Cover the staples and the join with masking tape.

JAGUAR AND EAGLE KNIGHTS

Ocelotl, the jaguar, is shown in this picture from a codex.

Warriors had to prove their bravery in battle and capture lots of prisoners for sacrifice. Those who succeeded were invited to join special fighting brotherhoods of jaguar and eagle knights. They wore costumes made of real feathers and skins.

WARRIOR SPIRIT

This stone carving is from the Maya city of Yaxchilan. In it, Lady Xoc, wife of ruler Shield Jaguar, kneels before a vision serpent. This serpent was made to appear by a special religious ritual. Maya rulers made offerings of their own blood to their ancestor-spirits and to the gods to ask for help in battle.

CLUBS AND SPEARS

Aztec soldiers face Spanish soldiers on horseback. They are armed with war-clubs called *macuahuitl* and protected by wooden shields.

War-clubs, made of wood and razor-sharp flakes of obsidian, could cut an enemy's head off with a single blow. The Spaniards are armed with metal swords and lances.

Fasten your eagle helmet by tying it under the chin. You could make wings from card and attach them to your arms with ribbon. Now you are a brave eagle knight! Eagles were admired by the Aztecs as superb hunters who could move freely to the Sun.

3 Make two eyes from self-drying clay and stick them on to the upper beak with glue. Neaten the edges of the beak and eyes with gummed paper tape.

4 Decorate both parts of the beak with paint. If you wish, add pieces of ribbon, felt or paper, too. Remember that you want to look brave and fierce.

5 Ask an adult to curl the feathers by running a scissor blade along them. Glue the layers of feathers on to the main feather decoration. Trim to fit.

6 Use tape and glue to fix feathers to the inside of the upper beak. Tape ribbon from the upper beak to the lower one to join. Leave some ribbon loose to tie.

Rival City-States

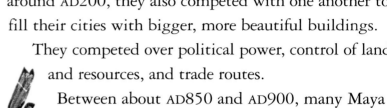

THE MAYA LIVED in many separate city-states, which were always rivals and sometimes at war. Rulers of different states fought to win more land. From around AD200, they also competed with one another to fill their cities with bigger, more beautiful buildings.

They competed over political power, control of land and resources, and trade routes.

Between about AD850 and AD900, many Maya cities became poorer, and their power collapsed. The great city centres were abandoned, and Maya scribes and craftworkers no longer carved important dates on temples and tombs. The last date known is AD889. No one knows why this happened. Perhaps it was because of famine, caused by bad weather or farmers over-using the land, or it may have been caused by war. However, Maya civilization did not totally disappear. A few Maya cities, in the far north and south of Mexico, continued to thrive.

Around AD900, the Putun people from the Gulf coast moved into Maya lands. In cities like Chichen-Itza, Putun ideas blended with Maya traditions to create a new culture.

TIKAL
This figure was painted on a pottery vase from the city of Tikal. From about AD600 to 900, Tikal was one of the greatest Maya city-states. It was wealthy, busy and very big. About 75,000 people lived there, and its buildings covered an area of 100 square kilometres. Around AD400, Tikal conquered the nearby Maya state of Uaxactun. Trading and religious links were then developed with the powerful non-Maya city of Teotihuacan.

CHICHEN-ITZA
Pilgrims came from miles around to throw jewellery and fine pottery into the Well of Sacrifice in the city of Chichen-Itza. These items were offerings to the god of rain. Human sacrifices were made here too. Chichen-Itza was founded by the Maya around AD800. Later, Maya craftsmen built a massive new city centre, with temples and ball-courts. Many of these new buildings were based on designs similar to those found in central Mexico. Some historians think this means that the city was conquered by the Putuns.

UXMAL
The city of Uxmal is in the dry Puuc region of Yucatan, Mexico. There are no rivers or streams in the area, so Maya engineers designed and built huge underground tanks, called *chultun*, to store summer rainfall. People living in Uxmal relied on these water tanks for survival.

NAMES AND DATES
This stone slab was once placed above a doorway in the Maya city of Yaxchilan. It is carved with glyphs, or picture-symbols, recording important names and dates. The city of Yaxchilan is famous for the fine quality stone carvings found there, especially on tall pillars and around doors.

PALENQUE
Lord Pacal, ruler of the Maya city of Palenque, was buried wearing this mask of green jade. Only the richest city-states could afford to bury their rulers with treasures like this. Palenque was at its strongest between AD600 and 800.

COPAN
This stela (tall stone pillar) is from Copan in modern Honduras. The front of the stela is carved with a larger-than-life portrait of 18 Rabbit (Waxaklahun ubah k'awil), the thirteenth ruler of the city. Archaeologists know much about Copan's past from the inscriptions carved in several monuments and buildings.

Aztec Conquests

TOTONAC TRIBUTE
Ambassadors from lands conquered by the Aztecs came to Tenochtitlan to deliver the tribute demanded from their rulers. This painting shows splendidly dressed representatives of the Totonac people meeting Aztec tax collectors. The Totonacs lived on the Gulf coast of Mexico, in Veracruz. Here they are shown offering tobacco, fruit and vanilla grown on their lands. They hated and feared the Aztecs.

WAR WAS ESSENTIAL to Aztec life. As newcomers in Mexico, the Aztecs had won their homeland by fighting against the people already living there. From then onwards, they relied on war to bring more land, new cities and extra tribute under their control. Without these riches won through war, the Aztec empire would have collapsed. Big cities such as Tenochtitlan needed steady supplies of tribute to feed their citizens. War was also a source of captives. The Aztecs believed that thousands of prisoners needed to be sacrificed each year.

Each new Aztec ruler had to start his reign with a battle. It was his duty to win fame and glory by conquering new territory and seizing enemy captives. During the 1400s, the Aztec empire grew rapidly, until the Aztecs ruled most of Mexico. This drive to conquer new territory was led by rulers Itzcoatl (1426–1440), Moctezuma Ilhuicamina (1440–1468) and Axayacatl (1468–1481). Conquered cities were often controlled by garrisons of Aztec soldiers and linked to the government in Tenochtitlan by large numbers of officials, such as tax collectors and scribes.

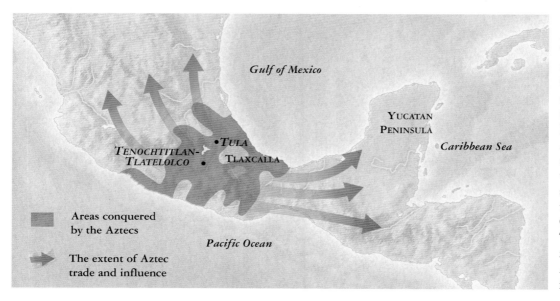

Gulf of Mexico

YUCATAN PENINSULA

Caribbean Sea

TENOCHTITLAN-
TLATELOLCO

•TULA
TLAXCALLA

Areas conquered
by the Aztecs

The extent of Aztec
trade and influence

Pacific Ocean

AZTEC LANDS
This map shows the area ruled by the Aztecs in 1519. Conquered cities were allowed to continue with their traditional way of life, but had to pay tribute to Aztec officials. The Aztecs also put pressure on two weaker city states, Texcoco and Tlacopan, to join with them in a Triple Alliance. One nearby city-state, Tlaxcalla, refused to make an alliance with the Aztecs and stayed fiercely independent.

CANNIBALS

One of the Aztecs' most important reasons for fighting was to capture prisoners for sacrifice. In this codex picture, we can see sacrificed bodies neatly chopped up. In some religious ceremonies, the Aztecs ate the arms and legs of sacrificed prisoners.

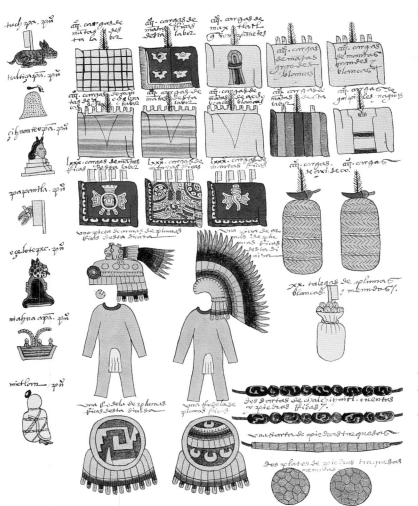

FROM HUMBLE BEGINNINGS

Aztec settlers are shown on their difficult trek through northern Mexico. The Aztecs built up their empire from humble beginnings in a short time. They first arrived in Mexico some time after AD1200. By around 1400, they had become the strongest nation in central Mesoamerica. To maintain their position, they had to be ready for war. The Aztecs invented many legends to justify their success. They claimed to be descended from earlier peoples living in Mexico, and to be specially guided by the gods.

TRIBUTE LIST

The Aztecs received vast quantities of valuable goods as tribute each year. Most of the tribute was sent to their capital city of Tenochtitlan. Aztec scribes there drew up very detailed lists of tribute received, like the one on the left. Among the goods shown are shields decorated with feathers, blankets, turquoise plates, bracelets and dried chilli peppers.

Scholars and Scribes

THE MAYA were the first – and only – Native American people to invent a complete writing system. Maya picture-symbols and sound-symbols were written in books, carved on buildings, painted on pottery and inscribed on precious stones. Maya scribes also developed an advanced number system, including a sign for zero, which Europeans at the time did not have.

Maya writing used glyphs (pictures standing for words) and also picture-signs that stood for sounds. The sound-signs could be joined together, like the letters of our alphabet, to spell out words and to make complete sentences. The Aztecs used picture-writing too, but theirs was much simpler and less flexible.

Maya and Aztec picture-symbols were very difficult to learn. Only specially trained scribes could write them and only priests or rich people could read them. They could spare time for study and afford to pay a good teacher.

MAYA READER

This Maya statue shows a wealthy woman, seated cross-legged with a codex (folding book), on her lap. A Maya or Aztec codex was made of long strips of fig-bark paper, folded like a concertina. The writing was read from top to bottom and left to right.

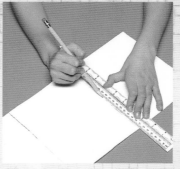

CITY EMBLEM

This is the emblem-glyph for the Maya city-state of Copan. It is made up of four separate images, which together give a message meaning "the home of the rulers of the royal blood of Copan". At the bottom, you can see a bat, the special picture-sign for the city.

MAKE A CODEX

You will need: thin card, ruler, pencil, scissors, white acrylic paint, eraser, large and small paintbrushes, water pot, paints in red, yellow, blue and black, palette, tracing paper.

1 Draw a rectangle about 100cm x 25cm on to thin card. Cut the rectangle out. Cover it evenly with white acrylic paint. Leave it to dry.

2 Using a pencil and ruler, lightly draw in four fold-lines 20cm apart. This will divide the painted card into five equal sections.

3 Carefully fold along the pencil lines to make a zig-zag book, as shown. Unfold the card and rub out the pencil lines with an eraser.

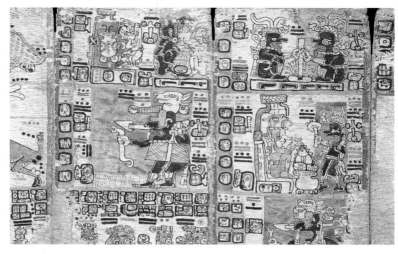

MAYA CODEX

Maya scribes wrote thousands of codices, but only four survive. All the rest were destroyed by Spanish missionaries. These pages from a Maya codex show the activities of several different gods. The figure at the top painted black with a long nose is Ek Chuah, the god of merchants.

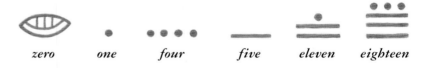

| zero | one | four | five | eleven | eighteen |

AZTEC ENCYCLOPEDIA

These pictures of Aztec gods come from a book known as the Florentine Codex. This encyclopedia was compiled between 1547 and 1569 by Father Bernardino de Sahagun, a Spanish friar. He was fascinated by Aztec civilization and wanted to record it before it disappeared. This codex is the most complete written record of Aztec life we have.

MAYA NUMBERS

The Maya number system used only three signs – a dot for one, a bar for five, and the shell-symbol for zero. Other numbers were made by using a combination of those signs. When writing down large numbers, Maya scribes put the different symbols on top of one another, rather than side by side as we do today.

4 Trace or copy Aztec or Maya codex drawings from this book. Alternatively, make up your own, based on Mesoamerican examples.

5 Paint your tracings or drawings, using light, bright colours. Using the Maya numbers on this page as a guide, add some numbers to your codex.

If you went to school in Aztec or Maya times, you would find out how to recognize hundreds of different picture-symbols. You would also be taught to link them together in your mind, like a series of clues, to find out what they meant.

Time, Sun and Stars

Like all other Mesoamericans, the Maya and the Aztecs measured time using a calendar with a year of 260 days. This was used in Mexico as early as 500BC and is probably based on human biology – 260 days is about how long it takes a baby to develop before it is born. The calendar was divided into 13 cycles of 20 days each. Mesoamerican farmers used a different calendar, based on the movements of the Sun, because sunlight and the seasons made their crops grow. This calendar had 360 days, divided into 18 months of 20 days, plus five extra days that were unlucky. Every 52 years, measured in our time, these two calendars ended on the same day. For five days before the end of the 52 years, people were anxious, because they feared the world might end. A third calendar, of 584 days, also existed for calculating festival days.

Sun Stone
This massive carving was made to display the Aztec view of creation. The Aztecs believed that the world had already been created and destroyed four times and that their Fifth World was also doomed.

Studying the Stars
The Caracol was constructed as an observatory to study the sky. From there, Maya astronomers could observe the planet Venus, which was important in the Mesoamericans' measurement of time.

Make a Sun Stone

You will need: pencil, scissors, thick card, self-drying clay, modelling tool, board, rolling pin, masking tape, PVA glue, glue brush, water bowl, pencil, thin card, water-based paints, paintbrush, water pot.

1 Cut a circle about 25cm in diameter from thick card. Roll out the clay and cut out a circle, using the card as a guide. Place the clay circle on the card one.

2 With a modelling tool, mark a small circle in the centre of the clay circle. Use a roll of masking tape as a guide. Do not cut through the clay.

3 Carve the Sun god's eyes, mouth, teeth and earrings. You can use the real Aztec Sun stone, shown at the top left of this page, as a guide.

alligator

wind

house

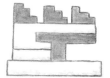
lizard

serpent

death's head

deer

rabbit

water

dog

monkey

grass

reed

jaguar

eagle

vulture

motion

flint knife

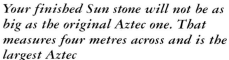
rain

flower

NAMES OF DAYS

These pictures from an Aztec codex show the 20 names for days from the farmers' calendar. These symbols were combined with a number from one to 13 to give the date, such as Three Vulture. The days were named after familiar creatures or everyday things, such as the lizard or water. Each day also had its own god. Children were often named after the day on which they were born, a custom that still continues in some parts of Mexico up to the present day.

Your finished Sun stone will not be as big as the original Aztec one. That measures four metres across and is the largest Aztec sculpture discovered so far.

4 Roll out more clay and cut out some Sun's rays, a tongue and eyebrows. Glue them to the clay circle. Smooth the edges with water and leave to dry.

5 Copy the 20 Aztec symbols (*above*) for days on to squares of thin card. The card squares should be no more than 2cm x 2cm. Cut out. Paint brown.

6 Cover the clay circle with a thin coat of dark brown paint. Leave it to dry. Then add a thin coat of white paint to make the circle look like stone.

7 Glue the card symbols evenly around the edge of the clay circle, as shown. Paint the Sun stone with a thin layer of PVA glue to seal and varnish it.

Gods and Goddesses

RELIGION WAS a powerful force throughout Mesoamerica. It affected everything people did, from getting up in the morning to digging in their fields or obeying their ruler's laws. Everyone believed that the gods governed human life. People could not fight their decisions, but the gods could sometimes be persuaded to grant favours if they were offered gifts and sacrifices. The Aztecs and Maya believed in ancient nature gods such as the fire god, the god of maize and the god of rain, and worshipped them with splendid festivals and ceremonies. Mesoamerican people also honoured the spirits of their dead rulers. The Aztecs had their own special tribal god, Huitzilopochtli, Lord of the Sun. He rewarded his followers with victories in war.

Religious ceremonies and sacrifices were led by temple priests. With long, matted hair, red-rimmed eyes and their painted bodies splattered with blood, they were a terrifying sight.

GOD OF SPRING
Xipe Totec was the Aztec god of fertility. He protected the young shoots of maize. Each year, captives were skinned alive as a sacrifice to him. Priests dressed in their skins in religious ceremonies to remind everyone of the skin of young plants.

CHACMOOL FIGURE
This stone statue from the city of Chichen-Itza shows a Chacmool, or reclining figure. It is holding a stone slab on which offerings may have been made.

A STATUE OF A GOD

You will need: pencil, paper, self-drying clay, modelling tool, pastry board, water bowl, petroleum jelly, cotton-wool bud, plaster of Paris, terracotta paint, small paintbrush.

1 Make a drawing of any Aztec god. Model it as a flat figure from self-drying clay. Keep it flat on the bottom. Leave the clay figure to dry.

2 Completely cover the surface of your model with petroleum jelly. Then smooth a layer of clay over the jelly, pressing it down gently into any grooves.

3 Spread more clay on top to make a strong rectangular block, at least 3cm thick. This will become your mould. Leave it to dry thoroughly.

WATER AND RAIN

Tlaloc was the Aztec god of life-giving rain, "the god who makes things grow". Under different names, he was worshipped throughout Mesoamerica. Tlaloc was honoured when he sent water to nourish the crops and feared when he sent deadly floods. In times of drought, the Aztecs sacrificed babies to Tlaloc. They believed the babies' tears would make rain fall.

SUN AND JAGUAR

This Maya carving was part of a wall at Campeche in south-eastern Mexico. It shows the Sun god, whom the Maya called Kinich Ahau. The Maya believed that he disappeared into the underworld every night, at sunset. It was there that he turned into a fierce jaguar god. At the beginning of every new day, they believed that Kinich Ahau then returned to Earth as the life-giving Sun.

EARTH MOTHER

This huge statue of Coatlicue (Great Lady Serpent Skirt) stood in the Sacred Precinct at Tenochtitlan. She was the fearsome Aztec earth-mother goddess. Coatlicue gave birth to the Aztecs' national god Huitzilopochtli, the Moon goddess, and the stars.

This model (right) is based on an Aztec statue. It shows a goddess holding two children. Figures of gods were often created from moulds (left).

4 Carefully ease the little model out of the solid block, using the modelling tool. The petroleum jelly should ensure that it comes away cleanly.

5 Clean any loose bits of clay from the mould and smear petroleum jelly inside. Use a cotton-wool bud to make sure the jelly is pushed into every part.

6 Mix up some plaster of Paris and pour it into the mould. Tap the mould gently to remove any air bubbles. Leave the plaster to dry for at least an hour.

7 Gently tip the plaster statue from the mould. Dust it with a brush, then paint it a terracotta colour, so that it looks like an Aztec pottery figure.

Temples and Sacrifices

MESOAMERICAN PEOPLE believed that unless they made offerings of blood and human lives to the gods, the Sun would die and the world would come to an end. Maya rulers pricked themselves with cactus thorns and sting-ray spines, or drew spiked cords through their tongues to draw blood. They pulled out captives' fingernails so the blood flowed or threw them into holy water-holes. Aztecs pricked their ear-lobes each morning and collected two drops of blood to give to the gods. They also went to war to capture prisoners. On special occasions, vast numbers of captives were needed for sacrifice. It was reported that 20,000 victims were sacrificed to celebrate the completion of the Great Temple at Tenochtitlan in 1487. It took four days to kill them all. Mesoamerican temples were tombs as well as places of sacrifice. Rulers and their wives were buried inside. Each ruler aimed to build a great temple as a memorial to his reign.

TEMPLE TOMB
Pyramid Temple 1 at Tikal was built in the AD700s as a memorial to a Maya king. Nine stone platforms were built above the burial chamber, to create a tall pyramid shape reaching up to the sky.

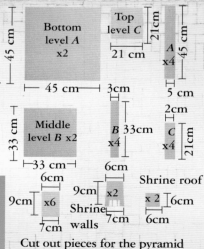

HOLY KNIFE
This sacrificial knife has a blade of a semi-precious stone called chalcedony. It was made by Mixtecs from south Mexico. Mesoamerican priests used finely decorated knives of flint, obsidian and other hard stones to kill captives for sacrifice. These were trimmed to be as sharp as glass.

A PYRAMID TEMPLE

You will need: pencil, ruler, thick card, scissors, PVA glue, glue brush, masking tape, thin strips of balsa wood, thin card, corrugated card, water bowl, paintbrushes, paints.

Bottom level *A* x2 — 45 cm, 45 cm

Top level *C* — 21 cm, 21 cm

A x4 — 45 cm, 5 cm

Middle level *B* x2 — 33 cm, 33 cm

B x4 — 33cm, 3cm

C x4 — 21cm, 2cm

Shrine walls — 9cm, x6, 7cm, 6cm

9cm, x2, 7cm, 6cm

Shrine roof — x 2, 6cm, 6cm

Cut out pieces for the pyramid and temple-top shrines from thick card, as shown above.

1 Use PVA glue and masking tape to join the thick card pieces to make three flat boxes (A, B and C). Leave the boxes until the glue is completely dry.

2 From the remaining pieces of card, make the two temple-top shrines, as shown. You could add extra details with strips of balsa wood or thin card.

SKULL SHRINE

Rows of human skulls, carved
in stone, decorate this shrine outside
the Aztecs' Great Temple in the centre of Tenochtitlan.
Most Aztec temples also had skull-racks, where rows of
real human heads were displayed. They were cut from
the bodies of sacrificed captives.

PERFECTION

The ideal victim
for human
sacrifice
was a fit
and healthy
young man.

RELIGIOUS GIFTS

Mesoamerican people
also made offerings of
food and flowers as gifts
to the gods. Maize was a
valuable gift because it was
the Mesoamerican people's
most important food. Bright
orange marigolds were a sign of the
Sun, on which every person's
life depended.

maize　　　　*marigolds*

HUMAN SACRIFICE

This Aztec codex painting
shows captives being sacrificed.
At the top, you can see a priest
cutting open a captive's chest
and removing the heart
as an offering to
the gods.

*This model is based on the
Great Temple that stood in
the centre of
Tenochtitlan.*

3 Glue the boxes, one on
top of the next. Cut out
pieces of card the same size
as each side of your boxes.
They should be about 1–2cm
wide. Stick down, as shown.

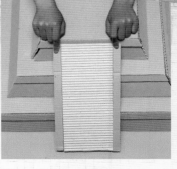

4 Cut out two strips of
card 2cm x 26cm. Glue
them to a third piece of
card 14cm x 26cm. Glue
corrugated card 9.5cm x
26cm in position, as shown.

5 Stick the staircase to
the front of the temple,
as shown. Use a ruler to
check that the staircase is
an equal distance from
either side of the temple.

7 Paint the whole temple
a cream colour to look
like natural stone. Add
details, such as carvings or
wall paintings, using
brightly coloured paint.

Time for Celebration

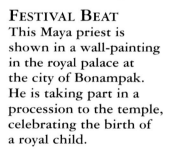

ESTIVALS, WITH MUSIC AND DANCING, were a very important part of Mesoamerican life. All big Aztec and Maya cities had a huge open space in the centre, where crowds gathered to sing and dance to honour the gods on festival days. Every twenty days, there were celebrations to mark the start of a new month. There were also festivals, with prayers and sacrifices, to mark important seasons of the farming year. In July and August, the Aztecs celebrated flowering trees and plants. In September, there were harvest festivals, and in October, festivals where hunters gave thanks for plentiful prey. For the Aztec rulers and their guests, feasts and entertainment were a regular event.

All of these special occasions involved music and song. Favourite instruments included rattles, whistles, ocarinas, flutes, bells and shells blown like trumpets. Aztec musicians also played a two-tone wooden drum, called a *teponaztli*, to provide a lively beat for dancing. Stringed instruments were unknown until after the Spanish conquest.

FESTIVAL BEAT
This Maya priest is shown in a wall-painting in the royal palace at the city of Bonampak. He is taking part in a procession to the temple, celebrating the birth of a royal child.

AN AZTEC ORCHESTRA
Musicians played conch shells, rattles and drums while crowds of worshippers sang and danced in the main square of Tenochtitlan.

AN AZTEC RATTLE

You will need: self-drying clay, modelling tool, pastry board, cling film, water bowl, dried melon seeds, bamboo cane, white and terracotta paint, paintbrush, water pot, feather, PVA glue, glue brush.

1 Make a solid model gourd from self-drying clay. You could copy the shape shown above. When it is dry, wrap the gourd completely in clingfilm.

2 Cover the wrapped model gourd with an outer layer of self-drying clay about 1cm thick. Smooth the clay with water to give an even surface.

3 Leave the outer layer of clay to get hard but not completely solid. Cut it in half with the thin end of the modelling tool and remove the model gourd.

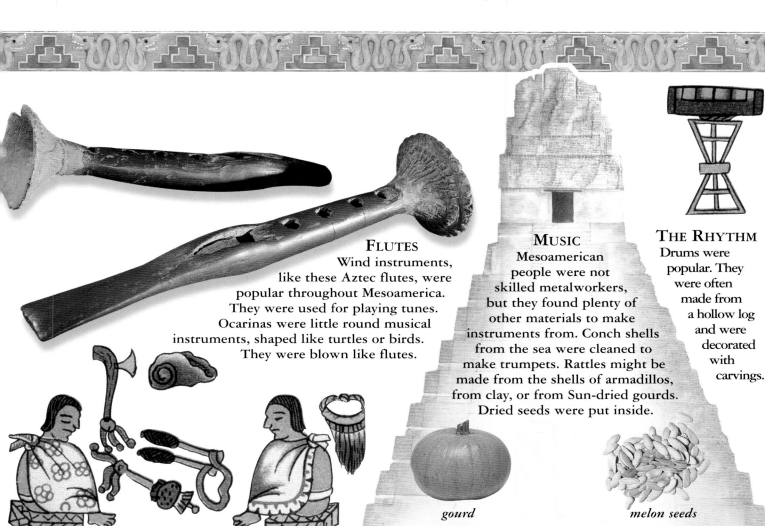

FLUTES

Wind instruments, like these Aztec flutes, were popular throughout Mesoamerica. They were used for playing tunes. Ocarinas were little round musical instruments, shaped like turtles or birds. They were blown like flutes.

MUSIC

Mesoamerican people were not skilled metalworkers, but they found plenty of other materials to make instruments from. Conch shells from the sea were cleaned to make trumpets. Rattles might be made from the shells of armadillos, from clay, or from Sun-dried gourds. Dried seeds were put inside.

gourd

melon seeds

THE RHYTHM

Drums were popular. They were often made from a hollow log and were decorated with carvings.

INSTRUMENTS

This picture from a codex shows two Aztec musicians with some of the instruments they played: a conch shell trumpet, dried-gourd rattles, and flutes made from clay. Some of the instruments are decorated with tassels and bows.

JUMPING FOR JOY

These pictures from an Aztec codex show a rattle-player, a drummer and a juggler. Acrobats, jugglers and contortionists performed at many joyful festivals, such as harvest-time celebrations.

4 Cover the edge of one half of the hollow gourd with wet clay. Put dry seeds or beans inside and a cane through the middle. Press the halves together.

5 When it is dry, decorate the rattle with painted patterns and push a feather into the top of the bamboo cane. Coat the rattle with PVA glue for a shiny finish.

Gourd-shaped rattles were very popular instruments in Mesoamerica. The seeds inside the dried gourds would provide the rattle sound. Codex pictures often show people carrying rattles in processions. The rattles were often decorated with feathers.

Sports and Games

MESOAMERICAN PEOPLE enjoyed sports and games after work and on festival days. Two favourite games were *tlachtli* or *ulama*, the famous Mesoamerican ball-game, and *patolli*, a board-game. The ball-game was played in front of huge crowds, while *patolli* was a quieter game. Mesoamerican games were not just for fun. Both the ball-game and *patolli* had religious meanings. In the first, the court symbolized the world, and the rubber ball stood for the Sun as it made its daily journey across the sky. Players were meant to keep the ball moving in order to give energy to the Sun. Losing teams were sometimes sacrificed as offerings to the Sun god. In *patolli*, the movement of counters on the board represented the passing years.

PATOLLI
A group of Aztecs are shown here playing the game of *patolli*. It was played by moving dried beans or clay counters along a cross-shaped board with 52 squares. It could be very exciting. Players often bet on the result.

THE ACROBAT
This Olmec statue shows a very supple acrobat. Mesoamericans admired youth, fitness and beauty. Sports were fun, but they could also be good training for the demands of war. Being fit was considered attractive.

FLYING MEN
Volador was a ceremony performed on religious festival days. Four men, dressed as birds and attached to ropes, jumped off a high pole. As they spun round, falling towards the ground, they circled the pole 13 times each. That made 52 circuits – the length of the Mesoamerican holy calendar cycle.

PLAY PATOLLI

You will need: thick card, pencil, ruler, black marker pen, paints, small paintbrush, water pot, coloured papers, scissors, PVA glue and glue brush, dried broad or butter beans, self-drying clay.

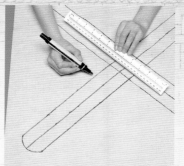

1 Measure a square of thick card about 50cm x 50cm. Using a marker pen and a ruler, draw three lines from corner to corner to make a cross-shape.

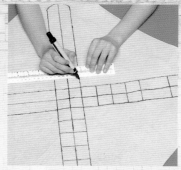

2 Draw seven pairs of spaces along each arm. The third space in from the end should be a double space. Paint triangles in it.

3 Draw eight jaguar heads and eight marigolds on differently coloured paper. Cut them out. Paint the face of the Sun god into the centre.

TARGET RING

This stone ring comes from Chichen-Itza. Ball-game players used only their hips and knees to hit a solid rubber ball through rings like this fixed high on the ball-court walls.

ALL DRESSED UP

A man dressed to play the Mesoamerican ball-game is shown in this terracotta statue. The figure was made around AD800 on the Maya island of Jaina, off the western coast of the Yucatan peninsula. He wears a protective belt of leather and wood, padded wrist-guards and knee-guards, a pointed cap and big earrings. Being a ball-game player was risky but could bring rich rewards. Winners were sometimes allowed to claim the spectators' clothes and jewels as prizes.

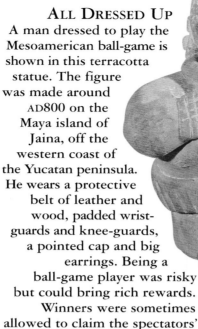

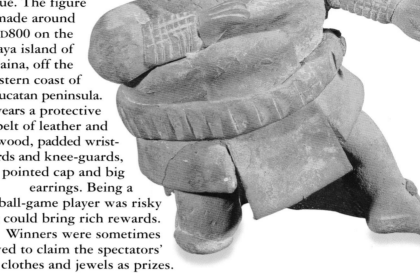

PLAY BALL

The ruins of a huge ball-court can still be seen in the Maya city of Uxmal. The biggest courts were up to 60m long and were built next to temples, in the centre of cities. People crowded inside the court to watch. Play was fast, furious and dangerous. Many players were injured as they clashed with opponents.

4 Stick the jaguars and marigolds randomly on the board. Paint a blue circle at the end of one arm, and a crown at the opposite end. Repeat in green on the other arms.

5 Paint five dried beans black with a white dot on one side. The beans will be thrown as dice. Make two counters from clay. Paint one green and one blue.

Most of the original rules for patolli have been lost. In this version, start each counter on the circle of the same colour. The aim is to move your counter to the crown of the same colour and back. Lose a turn if you land on a jaguar and get an extra turn if you land on a marigold.

The Coming of the Spanish

I N 1493 explorer Christopher Columbus arrived back in Spain from his pioneering voyage across the Atlantic Ocean. He told tales of an extraordinary "new world" full of gold. Excited by Columbus' stories, a group of Spanish soldiers sailed to Mexico in 1519, hoping to make their fortunes. They were led by a nobleman called Hernan Cortes. Together with the Aztecs' enemies, he led a march on Tenochtitlan. For the next two years, the Aztecs fought to stop Cortes and his soldiers taking over their land. At first, they had some success, driving the Spaniards out of Tenochtitlan in May 1520. Then, in 1521, Cortes attacked the city again, set fire to its buildings and killed around three-quarters of the population. In 1535, Mexico became a colony, ruled by officials sent from Spain.

A similar thing happened in Maya lands, but more slowly. The Spanish first landed there in 1523. They did not conquer the last independent city-state, Tayasal, until 1697.

AGAINST THE AZTECS
This picture comes from *The History of the Indies*. It was written by Diego Duran, a Spanish friar who felt sympathy for the Aztecs. Spanish soldiers and their allies from Tlaxcalla are seen fighting against the Aztecs. Although the Aztecs fought bravely, they had no chance of defeating Spanish soldiers mounted on horseback and armed with guns.

A SAD NIGHT
On 6 May 1520, Spanish soldiers massacred Aztecs gathered for a religious festival in Tenochtitlan. The citizens were outraged and attacked the Spaniards, many of whom died. During this night, the emperor Moctezuma II was stoned to death, probably by Aztecs who believed he had betrayed them. Cortes called this the *Noche Triste* (sad night).

THE END OF AZTEC POWER
This Aztec picture shows the surrender of Cuauhtemoc, the last Aztec king, to Cortes. After Moctezuma II died in 1520, the Aztecs were led by two of Moctezuma's descendants – Cuitlahuac, who ruled for only one year, and Cuauhtemoc. He was the last king and reigned until 1524.

RUNNING FOR THEIR LIVES

This illustration from a Spanish manuscript shows Aztec people fleeing from Spanish conquerors. You can see heavily-laden porters carrying stocks of food and household goods across a river to safety. On the far bank, mothers and children, with a pet bird and dog, hide behind huge maguey cactus plants.

WORKING LIKE SLAVES

Spanish settlers in Mexico took over all the Aztec and Maya fields and forced the people to work as farm labourers. They treated them cruelly, almost like slaves. This modern picture shows a Spanish overseer giving orders.

AFTER THE CONQUEST

Mexican artist Diego Rivera shows Mesoamerica after the Spanish conquest. Throughout the 1500s and 1600s, settlers from Spain arrived there. They drove out the local nobles and forced ordinary people to work for them. Spanish missionaries tried to replace local beliefs with European customs and Christianity. In Tenochtitlan, the Spaniards pulled down splendid Aztec palaces and temples to build churches and fine homes for themselves. You can see gangs of Aztec men working as labourers in the background of this picture.

Incas

From their capital city high in the Andes mountains, the Incas ruled a mighty empire that was home to over 20 different peoples. Farmers terraced steep mountain-sides to grow food crops. Labourers built huge stone temples, fortresses, and a vast network of roads. Craftworkers produced marvellous textiles that are unequalled today. Government officials controlled ordinary people's lives, but provided food, housing, and care in sickness or old age. The Incas created the most spectacular civilization ancient America had ever seen, rich in gold and treasures.

Peoples of the Andes

NOWY PEAKS AND GLACIERS rim the skyline above high, open plateaus. Cold lakes reflect the blue sky. These are the South American Andes, stretching for about 7,600km from Colombia to southern Chile. To the west, plains and deserts border the Pacific Ocean. To the east, steamy rainforests surround the Amazon River.

Humans settled here in about 11,000BC, or even earlier. Their ancestors crossed into North America from Asia and moved south. As the climate became warmer, tribes settled in the Andes and on the coast. They learned to farm and build villages. From about 1000BC, the seven civilizations of the Parácas, Chavín, Nazca, Moche, Tiwanaku, Wari and Chimú rose and fell. Last of all, from around AD1100 to 1532, came the Inca Empire.

IN THE HIGH ANDES
Alpacas cross a snowfield, high in the Andes. These woolly animals are related to the South American llama, guanaco and vicuña. Their wild ancestors may have been tamed in the Andes as early as 5400BC. Herding and farming were not essential for allowing great civilizations in the Andes, but the Incas developed these activities with great skill.

WORKERS OF GOLD
Hollow golden hands from a Chimú tomb may have been used as incense holders. The Chimú people came to power in northern Peru about 400 years before the Incas. Their smiths became very skilled at working gold. These craftsmen were later employed by the Incas.

DIGGING UP THE PAST
Archaeologists work near Sipán, in Peru's Lambayeque Valley. Burials of a warrior-priest and of Moche royalty, dating from about AD300, have been found there. The ancient Andean peoples kept no written records, so all we know of them comes from archaeology.

TIMELINE 11,000BC–AD1

Thousands of years before the Inca Empire was founded, people had settled on the Peruvian coast and in the Andes. The ruins of their cities and temples still stood in Inca times. They were part of the Inca world.

*c.*11,000BC People settle at Monte Verde, Chile.

*c.*10,000BC Stone tools are in use in Peru.

*c.*9000BC The climate becomes warmer, and glaciers retreat.

*c.*8600BC Beans, bottle gourds and chilli peppers are cultivated.

*c.*7500BC Guanaco, vicuña and deer become common in the Andes and are hunted for food.

*c.*5400BC Alpacas, and probably llamas, are herded.

Farming spreads along the coast and in the highlands.

*c.*4500BC Andean farmers cultivate squash.

stone tools

llama

*c.*3800BC Maize, manioc and cotton are grown in the Andes.

*c.*3500BC Llamas are used as pack animals to transport goods.

*c.*3200–1500BC Mummification is used to preserve the bodies of dead people in the north of Chile.

*c.*2800BC Pottery is made in Ecuador and in Colombia.

*c.*2600BC Temples are built on platform mounds on the Peruvian coast.

11,000BC   8600BC   3800BC   2500

VALLEY OF MYSTERY
The Urubamba River winds through steep, forested gorges. In 1911, an American archaeologist called Dr Hiram Bingham came to the area in search of Inca ruins. He discovered a lost city on the slopes of Machu Picchu, high above the river valley.

NAZCA PUZZLES
Mysterious markings on the ground were scraped on the desert on a gigantic scale by the Nazca people. Their civilization grew up on the coast of southern Peru, a thousand years before the Incas. The lines may have marked out routes for religious processions.

ANCIENT PEOPLES
This man is one of the Aymara people who live around Lake Titicaca, on the high border between Peru and Bolivia. Some historians believe they are descended from the builders of a great city called Tiwanaku. Others say that they arrived from the Cañete Valley after Tiwanaku was abandoned in about 1250. Although their way of life has changed over the ages, the Aymara have kept a distinctive identity.

IN SOUTH AMERICA
The great civilizations of South America grew up in the far west of the continent. The area is now occupied by the modern countries of Colombia, Ecuador, Peru, Bolivia, Chile and Argentina.

---

*c.*2500BC A temple with stepped platforms is built at El Paraíso on the coast of Peru.

Backstrap looms are used.

Potatoes and *quinua* are cultivated.

There is widespread fishing along the Peruvian coast and the northern coast of Chile.

quinua   Andean farmers use irrigation.

backstrap loom

*c.*2000BC The farming of maize, which first developed on the south-central coast and the north coast, is now widespread along the Peruvian coast and in the highlands.

*c.*1800BC Pottery-making develops along the coast of Peru.

*c.*1500BC Metal-working develops in Peru.

*c.*1000BC Large-scale settlement takes place in the Andes.

*c.*900BC The Chavín culture develops. The temple complex at Chavín de Huantar is built.

*c.*700BC The Parácas culture begins to thrive.

*c.*200BC The Chavín culture comes to an end.

The Nazca culture develops on the coast of southern Peru. Gigantic Nazca lines are marked on the surface of the deserts.

Chavín stone head

The Great Empire

WHO WERE THE INCAS and where did they come from? If you had asked them, they would have told you proudly that their first great ruler, Manko Qapaq, was sent to Earth by his father Inti, the Sun. Manko Qapaq's queen, Mama Okllo, was believed to be the daughter of the Moon.

The Incas believed that they were superior to all other peoples. In reality, they were just the last link in a long chain of civilizations. They shared many beliefs with these peoples, often taking over their technology and crafts. From their mountain homeland, they learned how to live in the same landscapes and make use of them, ruling coast, desert and rainforest. The Incas started out as just one of many small tribes living in the Peruvian Andes in the 1100s. In the 1300s, led by their ruler Mayta Qapaq, they began to conquer neighbouring lands. During the 1400s, Inca armies and officials created a huge Empire. Although the Incas themselves only numbered about 40,000, they ruled a total population of about 12 million. Of the 20 languages that were spoken in the Inca Empire, the most important was Quechua, which is still widely spoken in the Andes mountains today.

This vast Empire seemed as if it would last for ever. In 1532, something happened to change that. Spanish soldiers landed in Peru, greedy for gold and land.

TAWANTINSUYU
The Incas called their Empire Tawantinsuyu (the Four Quarters). This name referred to the regions of Chinchaysuyu, Collasuyu, Antisuyu and Cuntisuyu (North, South, East and West). Their borders met at Cuzco, the capital, known as the "navel of the world". At the height of its power, during the 1400s, Tawantinsuyu stretched 3,600km from north to south, and about 320km inland across the Andes. This immense Empire took in the lands that now make up Peru, northern Chile, the far west of Argentina, part of Bolivia, Ecuador and the southern borders of Colombia.

M*e*
stir
spo

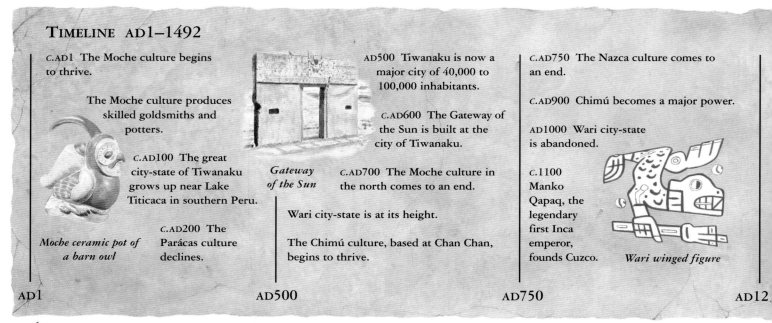

TIMELINE AD1–1492

*C.*AD1 The Moche culture begins to thrive.

The Moche culture produces skilled goldsmiths and potters.

*C.*AD100 The great city-state of Tiwanaku grows up near Lake Titicaca in southern Peru.

Moche ceramic pot of a barn owl

*C.*AD200 The Parácas culture declines.

Gateway of the Sun

AD500 Tiwanaku is now a major city of 40,000 to 100,000 inhabitants.

*C.*AD600 The Gateway of the Sun is built at the city of Tiwanaku.

*C.*AD700 The Moche culture in the north comes to an end.

Wari city-state is at its height.

The Chimú culture, based at Chan Chan, begins to thrive.

*C.*AD750 The Nazca culture comes to an end.

*C.*AD900 Chimú becomes a major power.

AD1000 Wari city-state is abandoned.

*C.*1100 Manko Qapaq, the legendary first Inca emperor, founds Cuzco.

Wari winged figure

AD1   AD500   AD750   AD12.

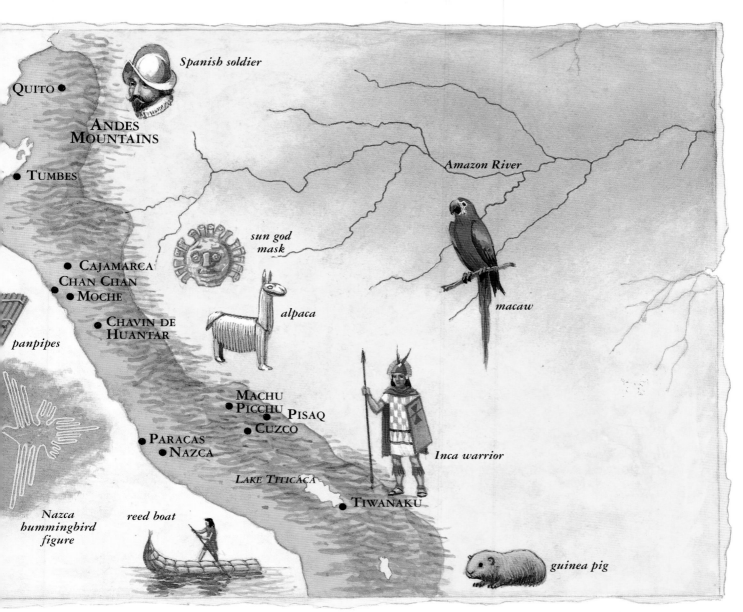

Spanish soldier

QUITO

ANDES
MOUNTAINS

TUMBES

Amazon River

sun god
mask

CAJAMARCA
CHAN CHAN
MOCHE

CHAVIN DE
HUANTAR

alpaca

macaw

panpipes

MACHU
PICCHU
PISAQ
CUZCO

PARACAS
NAZCA

Inca warrior

LAKE TITICACA

Nazca
hummingbird
figure

reed boat

TIWANAKU

guinea pig

---

*c.*1250 The once-great city of
Tiwanaku is abandoned, perhaps
because of changes in the climate.

*c.*1300 Sinchi Roka is the first
emperor to use the title *Sapa Inca.*

1370 Chimor, the Empire of
the Chimú people, expands.

*c.*1410 The Incas make new alliances
under the emperor Wiraqocha.

1437 Wiraqocha's son Yupanki conquers
the mountain State of Chanca.

*Chimú gold
funeral mask*

1438 Wiraqocha backs another
son, Urqon, as the
next emperor.

Yupanki proclaims himself
emperor of a rival Inca State and
renames himself Pachakuti.

Urqon is killed, and his father
Wiraqocha dies.

The Inca State is reunited under Pachakuti.

*c.*1440 The powerful emperor,
Minchançaman, rules Chimú.

*c.*1445 Pachakuti's brother,
Qapaq Yupanki, explores the
coastline to the south.

*c.*1450 Incas build Machu
Picchu high in the Andes.

1450 The Inca Empire grows
by conquest. Cuzco is rebuilt.

1470 Incas conquer Chimor.

1471 Topa Inka Yupanki
becomes emperor. A great
age of road building begins.

*Chimú
ritual knife*

AD1438

AD1445

AD1492

69

Makers of History

BECAUSE INCA HISTORY was not written down at the time, much of it has to be pieced together from chronicles and diaries recorded in the years after the Spanish conquest in the 1500s. Many accounts describe the everyday lives of ordinary people in the days of the Inca Empire. The names of the people who dug the fields and built the roads are mostly forgotten. Only the names of the Inca royal family and the nobles are known.

The first eight emperors recalled in Inca folklore probably did exist. However over the centuries their life stories, passed on from parent to child over generations, became mixed up with myths and legends. The last 100 years of Inca rule, beginning when Pachakuti Inka Yupanki came to the throne in 1438, were fresh in people's memories when the Spanish invaded. As a result, we know a good deal about the greatest days of the Inca Empire.

MAMA OKLLO
This painting from the 1700s imagines the Inca empress, Mama Okllo, carrying a Moon mask. She reigned in the 1100s. In some Inca myths, she and her brother Manko Qapaq were said to be the children of the Sun and the Moon. Mama Okllo married her brother, who became the first ruler of the Incas. They had a son called Sinchi Roka.

ON THE ROAD TO RUIN
An Inca emperor and empress are carried around their Empire. The Inca rulers had almost unlimited power, but were destroyed by bitter rivalry within the royal family. When the Spanish invaders arrived in 1532, Tawantinsuyu was divided between supporters of Waskar and his brother Ataw Wallpa.

TIMELINE AD1492–1781

1492 The Incas conquer northern Chile.

1493 Wayna Qapaq becomes emperor.

1498 Wayna Qapaq conquers part of Colombia and the Inca Empire reaches its greatest extent.

*c.*1523 A ship-wrecked Spaniard called Alejo García enters Inca territory from the east with raiding Chiriquana warriors. He dies during his return journey.

quipu used for government records

1525 Wayna Qapaq dies without an agreed successor. His son Waskar is chosen and crowned as the twelfth *Sapa Inca* in Cuzco. Waskar's brother, Ataw Wallpa, claims the imperial throne.

War breaks out in the Inca Empire as the brothers battle for power.

1526–7 A Spanish naval expedition sights Inca rafts off the Pacific coast.

Inca warrior

1529 The Spanish king approves a plan by Francisco Pizarro to conquer Peru.

1532 Waskar is defeated by his brother Ataw Wallpa.

The Spanish, under Francisco Pizarro, enter the inland city of Cajamarca and kill 7,000 Incas.

1533 Ataw Wallpa and his sister, Asarpay, are killed by the Spanish.

Inca rope bridge

AD1492   AD1525   AD1529   AD15

LLOQE YUPANKI

The son of Sinchi Roka, Lloqe Yupanki was chosen to be ruler of the lands around Cuzco in place of his older brother. He was a wise ruler, and his reign in the 1200s was peaceful. His son Mayta Qapaq was more warlike. He expanded his Empire by conquering neighbouring peoples.

PACHAKUTI INKA YUPANKI (REIGNED 1438–71)

Inka Yupanki was still a prince when he proved himself in war by conquering the Chanca people. However, his father Wiraqocha chose another son, Inka Urqon, as the next emperor. Yupanki claimed the throne, calling himself Pachakuti, which means "the world turned upside down". Urqon was killed, and his father died soon after.

ATAW WALLPA (REIGNED 1532–3)

Known as Atahuallpa or Atabaliba to the Spanish, Ataw Wallpa was the son of the great emperor Wayna Qapaq, who died unexpectedly in 1525. When his brother Waskar was crowned in Cuzco, Ataw Wallpa stayed with the army in the north, and a bitter war followed. By 1532, Waskar had been imprisoned, and Ataw Wallpa was ruler. But before the Empire could recover from the war, the Spanish invaded. Ataw Wallpa was captured and executed the following summer.

FRANCISCO PIZARRO (C.1478–1541)

In 1532, this Spanish soldier sailed to the Inca city of Tumbes with just 180 men and 37 horses. They marched inland to Cajamarca. Pizarro used treachery to capture and kill the Inca emperor, Ataw Wallpa. This army went on to loot Inca gold and bring Peru under Spanish rule. Resistance from the local people was fierce – but not as fierce as the rivalry and greed of the Spanish. Pizarro was murdered by one of his fellow countrymen fewer than ten years later.

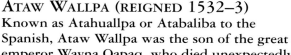

1535 The Incas rebel against Spain.

1536 Incas lay siege to the city of Cuzco. The city is burnt to the ground by the Incas.

The Inca Empire collapses.

1537 A last Inca State is formed by Cura Okllo and Manko Inka, based at Vilcabamba.

1538 The Spanish invaders fight among themselves at Las Salinas, near Cuzco.

Inca messenger with conch shell

1539 Cura Okllo, the successor to Asarpay and the sister-wife of Manko Inka, is executed by the Spanish.

1541 Pizarro is assassinated.

1545 Manko Inka is assassinated.

1572 Inca resistance under Tupac Amaru I is finally defeated, and he is executed. He is the last Inca ruler.

Vilcabamba and Machu Picchu are abandoned.

1742 Resistance to the Spanish grows. Calls for restoration of the Inca Empire.

1780 Major uprising of indigenous peoples under José Gabriel Condorcanqui He adopts the name of his ancestor and declares himself Tupac Amaru II. He aims to restore the Inca Empire.

1781 Tupac Amaru II is captured and horribly tortured to death.

Spanish conquistador

AD1539   AD1742   AD1781

Lords of the Sun

MANY OF THE EARLY TRIBES that lived in the Andes and on the Pacific coast were small groups of hunters and farmers. As cities and kingdoms grew in size, they began to need strong leadership. By about AD900, the State of Chimor was headed by powerful kings.

The Inca emperor was called *Sapa Inca* (Only Leader). As a descendant of the Sun, he was regarded as a god. He had complete power over his subjects, but he always had to be on his guard. There were many rivals for the throne among his royal relations. Each emperor had a new palace built for himself in the royal city of Cuzco. Emperors were treated with the utmost respect at all times and were often veiled or screened from ordinary people.

The empress, or *Quya* (Star), was the emperor's sister or mother. She was also thought to be divine and led the worship of the Moon goddess. The next emperor was supposed to be chosen from among her sons. An emperor had many secondary wives. Waskar was said to have fathered eighty children in just eight years.

RELIGIOUS LEADERS
Sacrifices of llamas were made to the gods each month, at special festivals and before battle. The *Sapa Inca* controlled all religious activities. In the 1400s, the emperor Wiraqocha Inka declared that worship of the god Wiraqocha, the Creator (after whom he was named), was more important than worship of Inti, the Sun god. This made some people angry.

A CHOSEN WOMAN
Young girls, the *akllakuna*, were educated for four years in religious matters, weaving and housekeeping. Some became the emperor's secondary wives or married noblemen. Others became priestesses or *mamakuna* (virgins of the Sun). Figurines like these wore specially made clothes, but these have perished or been lost over the years.

A FEATHER FAN
You will need: pencil, card, ruler, scissors, paints in bright colours, paintbrush, water pot, masking tape, wadding, PVA glue, hessian or sackcloth, needle, thread, string or twine.

1 Draw a feather shape 18cm long on to card and cut it out. The narrow part should be half of this length. Draw around the shape on card nine times.

2 Carefully paint the feathers with bright colours. Use red, orange and yellow to look like rainforest birds. Allow the paint to dry completely.

3 Cut out each feather and snip along the sides of the widest part to give a feathery effect. When the paint is dry, paint the other side as well.

COMMANDER IN CHIEF

The emperor sits on his throne. He wears a tasselled woollen headdress or *llautu*, decorated with gold and feathers, and large gold earplugs. He carries a sceptre. Around him, army chiefs await their orders. Emperors played an active part in military campaigns and relied on the army to keep them in power.

COOL SPRINGS

At Tambo Machay, to the south of Cuzco, fresh, cold water is channelled from sacred springs. Here, the great Pachakuti Inka Yupanki would bathe after a hard day's hunting.

THE LIVING DEAD

The dead body of an emperor, preserved as a mummy, is paraded through the streets. When each emperor died, his palace became his tomb. Once a year, the body was carried around Cuzco amid great celebrations. The picture is by Guamán Poma de Ayala, who was of Inca descent. In the 1600s, he made many pictures of Inca life.

Feathers from birds of the tropical forests to the east of the Andes were used to make fans for the emperor.

4 Hold the narrow ends of the feathers and spread out the tops to form a fan shape. Use masking tape to secure the ends firmly in position.

5 Cut a rectangular piece of wadding 9cm high and long enough to wrap the base of the feathers several times. Use glue on one side to keep it in place.

6 Cut a strip of hessian or sackcloth about 5cm wide. Starting at the base of the feathers, wrap the fabric around the stems. Hold it in place with a few stitches.

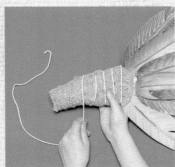

7 Wind string or twine firmly around the hessian to form the fan's handle. Tuck in the ends and use glue at each end to make sure they are secure.

The Inca State

FAMILY CONNECTIONS PLAYED an important part in royal power struggles and in everyday social organization in the Inca world. The nobles were grouped into family-based corporations called *panakas*. Members of each *panaka* shared rights to an area of land, its water, pasture and herds. Linked to each *panaka* was a land-holding *ayllu* (or clan) – a group of common people who were also related to each other.

The Incas managed to control an empire that contained many different peoples. Loyal Incas were sent to live in remote areas, while troublemakers from the regions were resettled nearer Cuzco, where they could be carefully watched. Conquered chiefs were called *kurakas*. They and their children were educated in Inca ways and allowed to keep some of their local powers.

The Inca system of law was quite severe. State officials and *kurakas* (conquered chiefs) acted as judges. Those who stole from the emperor's stores of grain, textiles and other goods faced a death sentence. Torture, beating, blinding and exile were all common punishments. The age of the criminal and the reason for the crime were sometimes taken into account.

A CLEVER CALCULATOR
One secret of Inca success was the *quipu*. It was used by government officials for recording all kinds of information, from the number of households in a town to the amount of goods of various kinds in a warehouse. The *quipu* was a series of strings tied to a thick cord. Each string had one or more colours and could be knotted. The colours represented anything from types of grain to groups of people. The knots represented numbers.

ONE STATE, MANY PEOPLES
The ancestors of these Bolivian women were subjects of the Incas. The Inca Empire was the largest ever known in all the Americas. It included at least a hundred different peoples. The Incas were clever governors and did not always try to force their own ideas upon other groups. Conquered peoples had to accept the Inca gods, but they were allowed to worship in their own way and keep their own customs.

A ROYAL INSPECTION

Topa Inka Yupanki inspects government stores in the 1470s. In the Inca world, nearly all grain, textiles and other goods were produced for the State and stored in warehouses. Some extra produce might be bartered, or exchanged privately, but there were no big markets or shops.

PUBLIC WORKS

Labourers build fortifications on the borders of the Inca Empire. People paid their taxes to the Inca State in the form of labour called *mit'a*. This might be general work on the land. Men were also conscripted to work on public buildings or serve in the army. The Spanish continued to operate the *mit'a* as a form of tax long after they conquered the Inca Empire.

OLLANTAYTAMBO

This building in Ollantaytambo, in the Urubamba Valley, was once a State storehouse for the farm produce of the region. Ollantaytambo was a large town, which was probably built about 550 years ago. It protected the valley from raids by the warriors who lived in the forests to the east. Buildings dating from the Inca Empire were still being lived in by local people when the American archaeologist Dr Hiram Bingham passed through in 1911.

Nobles and Peasants

INCA SOCIETY was strictly graded. At the top were the *Sapa Inca* and his *Quya*. The High Priest and other important officials were normally recruited from members of the royal family.

If noblemen were loyal to the emperor, they might receive gifts of land. They might be given gold or a beautiful *akllakuna* as a wife. They could expect jobs as regional governors, generals or priests. Lords and ladies wore fine clothes and were carried in splendid chairs, called litters.

Next in rank were the conquered non-Inca rulers and chiefs, the *kurakas*. They were cleverly brought into the Inca political system and given traditional honours. They served as regional judges.

Most people in the Empire were peasants. They were unable to leave their villages without official permission. They had no choice but to stay and toil on the land, sending their produce to the government stores.

CRAFT AND CLASS
A pottery figure from the Peruvian coast shows a porter carrying a water pot on his back. In the Inca Empire, craft workers such as potters and goldsmiths were employed by the State. They formed a small middle class. Unlike peasants they were never made to do *mit'a* (public service).

A MOCHE NOBLEMAN
The man's face on this jar is that of a noble. It was made by a Moche potter on the north coast of Peru between 1,500 and 2,000 years ago. The man's headdress sets him apart as a noble, perhaps a high priest.

A WATER POT
You will need: self-drying clay, cutting board, rolling pin, ruler, water, water pot, acrylic paints, paintbrush.

1 Roll out a piece of clay on the board. Make a circle about 17cm in diameter and 1cm thick. This will form the base of your water pot.

2 Roll some more clay into long sausages, about as fat as your little finger. Dampen the base with water and carefully place a sausage around the edge.

3 Coil more clay sausages on top of each other to build up the pot. Make each coil slightly smaller than the one below. Water will help them stick.

A PEASANT'S LIFE

A woman harvests potatoes near Sicuani, to the south of Cuzco. Then, as now, life was hard for the peasant farmers of the Andes. Both men and women worked in the fields, and even young children and the elderly were expected to help. However, the Inca State did provide some support for the peasants, supplying free grain in times of famine.

PLUGGED IN

This Chimú earplug is made of gold, turquoise and shell. It was worn as a badge of rank. Inca noblemen wore such heavy gold earplugs that the Spanish called them *orejones* (big ears). Noblewomen wore their hair long, covered with a head-cloth.

LAND AND SEASONS

One third of all land and produce belonged to the emperor, one third to the priests and one third to the peasants. It was hardly a fair division. A peasant's life, digging, planting and harvesting, was ruled by the seasons. Each new season was celebrated by religious festivals and ceremonies.

Children were expected to help their parents by fetching water from the wells and mountain springs.

4 When you reach the neck of the pot, start making the coils slightly bigger again to form a lip. Carefully smooth the coils with wet fingertips.

5 Use two more rolls of clay to make handles on opposite sides of the pot. Smooth out the joints carefully to make sure the handles stay in place.

6 Leave the clay to dry completely. Then paint the pot all over with a background colour. Choose an earthy reddish brown to look like Inca pottery.

7 Leave the reddish brown colour to dry. Use a fine paintbrush and black paint to draw Inca designs on the pot like the ones in the picture above.

On Land and Water

PERU TODAY is still criss-crossed by the remains of cobbled roads built by the Incas. Two main paved highways ran north to south, one following the coast and the other following the Andes. The first was about 3,600km long, the second even longer. The two roads were joined by smaller roads linking towns and villages. The roads crossed deserts, mountains and plateaus. Markers measured out distances in *topos*, units of about 7km.

Despite these great engineering works, most people in the Empire were not allowed to travel at all. These fine roads were strictly for use by people on official business. Messages to and from the emperor were carried by trained relay runners called *chasquis*, who were stationed in stone shelters along the way. In one day, a message could travel 240km. Government rest-houses called *tambos* were built on the chief routes.

The Incas were very inventive, but they had no wheeled transport. Baggage and goods were carried by porters or on the backs of llamas. Nobles travelled in richly decorated litters, carried by four or more men.

THE WATER CARRIER
A porter carries a jar on his head. Steep mountain roads must have made such work very tiring. The State road network allowed crops, food, drink, precious metal ores and textiles to be brought to the royal court from far-flung regions of the Empire.

TRAVELLING TO WAR
A litter, carried at shoulder height by four strong men, carries the emperor Wayna Qapaq to war. One purpose of the Inca road network was to make sure that armies could be moved quickly from one end of the Empire to the other. Depots and food stores for army use were built along the highways. Depot managers were kept in a state of readiness by royal officials.

THE ROAD GOES ON
An old Inca road zigzags up steep, terraced slopes near Pisaq. Inca engineers laid down about 16,000km of roads in all. Some highway sections were up to 7m across. Most were just broad enough for a llama – about 1m wide. The steepest sections were stepped.

BOATS OF REEDS
These modern boats were made by the Uru people of Lake Titicaca. The Incas made boats and rafts for travel on lakes, rivers and the ocean. Because there was a shortage of timber in most areas, they made them from a type of reed, called *totora*. These were cut, trimmed and tightly bound in bundles. They were light, buoyant and strong, and could be bent into curved shapes to form the prow and stern of a boat.

HIGHWAY PATROL
The governor of bridges watches as a porter carrying goods on his back crosses a rope bridge across a mountain river. Bridges had to be able to take considerable stress and strain, caused by the tramp of marching armies and by hundreds of heavily burdened llamas. Officials inspected roads and bridges and could order local workers to repair them under the *mit'a* system of conscripted labour.

BRIDGES OF ROPE
Rope bridges are still made from plaited mountain grasses by the Quechua people. This one crosses a gorge of the Apurimac River in Peru. Inca engineers built long rope bridges like this one, as well as stone bridges, causeways over marshy ground and tunnels through rock. Sometimes people crossed rivers in baskets hauled across the water on ropes.

Master Masons

THE ROCKS of the Andes mountains provided high quality granite that was used for impressive public buildings. These included temples, fortresses, palaces, holy shrines and aqueducts (stone channels for carrying water supplies).

The *mit'a* labour system provided the workforce. In the quarries, massive rocks weighing up to 120 tonnes were cracked and shifted with stone hammers and bronze crowbars. They were hauled with ropes on log rollers or sleds. On site, the stones were shaped to fit and rubbed smooth with water and sand. Smaller stone blocks were used for upper walls or lesser buildings.

The expert Inca stonemasons had only basic tools. They used plumblines (weighted cords) to make sure that walls were straight. They used no mortar or cement, but the stones fitted together perfectly. Many remain in place to this day. Most public buildings were on a grand scale, but all were of a simple design.

BUILDING THE TEMPLE
These rectangular stone blocks were part of the holiest site in the Inca Empire, the *Coricancha* (Temple of the Sun). Inca stonework was deliberately designed to withstand the earthquakes that regularly shake the region. The original temple on this site was badly damaged by a tremor in 1650.

BRINGER OF WATER
This beautifully engineered stone water-channel was built across a valley floor by Inca stonemasons. Aqueducts, often covered, were used both for irrigation and for drinking supplies. Irrigation schemes were being built in Peru as early as around 4,500 years ago.

AN INCA GRANARY
You will need: ruler, pencil, beige, dark and cream card, scissors, white pencil, paints, paintbrush, water pot, pair of compasses, masking tape, PVA glue, hay or straw.

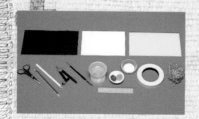

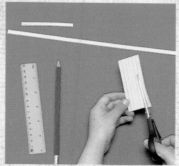

1 Use a ruler and pencil to mark eight strips 8.5cm long and 0.25cm wide, and one strip 36cm long and 0.25cm wide on beige card. Cut them out.

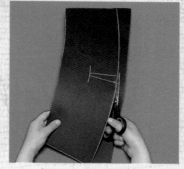

2 On the dark card, draw a curved shape 34cm along the base, 11cm in height and 30cm along the top. Cut it out. Cut out a doorway 6cm high.

3 Paint another piece of card a stone colour. Leave it to dry. Cut it into "blocks" about 2cm high. Glue them one by one on to the building shape.

HISTORY IN STONE

Stone walls and streets, such as these fine examples still standing in Ollantaytambo, survive to tell a story. Archaeology is much more difficult in the rainforests to the east, where timber structures rot rapidly in the hot, moist air. That is one reason we know more about the way people lived in the Andes than in the Amazon region.

A MASSIVE FORTRESS

Llamas still pass before the mighty walls of Sacsahuaman, at Cuzco. This building was a fortress with towers and terraces. It also served as a royal palace and a sacred shrine. Its multi-sided boulders are precisely fitted. It is said to have been built over many years by 30,000 labourers. It was one of many public buildings raised in the reign of Pachakuti Inka Yupanki.

INCA DESIGN

A building in Machu Picchu shows an example of typical Inca design. Inca stonemasons learned many of their skills from earlier Peruvian civilizations. Openings that are wider at the bottom than the top are seen only in Inca buildings. They are said to be trapezoid.

Storehouses were built of neat stone blocks. They kept precious grain dry and secure.

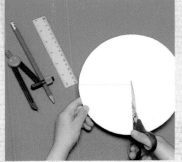

4 Use compasses to draw a circle 18cm across on cream card. Cut it out and cut away one quarter. Tape the straight cut edges together to form a cone.

5 Make a circle by joining the ends of the 36cm strip with masking tape. Then fix the eight 8.5cm strips around the edge and in the middle as shown.

6 Glue short lengths of straw or hay all over the cardboard cone to form the thatched roof of the granary. The thatch should all run in the same direction.

7 Join the edges of the walls with masking tape. Fold in the sides of the doorway. Place the rafters on top. The thatched roof fits over the rafters.

Town Dwellers

WATER ON TAP
At Machu Picchu, water was channelled into the town from the mountain springs that bubbled up about 1.5km outside the city walls. The water ran into stone troughs and fountains, and it was used for bathing and drinking.

GREAT CITIES had been built in Peru long before the Incas came to power. In about AD600, the city of Tiwanaku, near Lake Titicaca, may have had a population of nearly 100,000. A hundred years later, the Chimú capital of Chan Chan covered 15 square kilometres of the coastal plain.

The Inca capital, Cuzco, was ringed by mountains and crossed by two rivers that had been turned into canals, the Huatanay and the Tullamayo. Cuzco became dominated by fine public buildings and royal palaces when it was rebuilt in about 1450. At its centre was the great public square, known as *Waqaypata* (Holy Place). At festival time, this square was packed with crowds. Roads passed from here to the four quarters of the Empire. They were lined by the homes of Inca nobles, facing in upon private compounds called *canchas*. The centre of the city was home to about 40,000 people, but the surrounding suburbs and villages housed a further 200,000. Newer Inca towns, such as Pumpo, Huanuco and Tambo Colorado, were planned in much the same way as Cuzco, but adapted to the local landscape.

THE PAST REVEALED
Archaeologists record every detail of what they find with the greatest care. Here at an old Inca town near Cuzco, they are using precision instruments to note the exact position of everything they uncover. Excavations in Inca towns have unearthed pots and jars, fragments of cloth, jewellery, knives and human burials. They are constantly adding to what we know about the Inca civilization.

STEEP STREETS
Machu Picchu was built on a steep slope, using *mit'a* labour. Some of its buildings were set into the rock, while many more were built on raised terraces of stone. Its streets had steps in many places. Incas may have fled to this mountain retreat from Cuzco after the Spanish invaded in 1532. It was abandoned within 40 years and soon covered by creepers and trees.

RUINS OF CHAN CHAN

Chan Chan, capital of Chimor, was built in the north, at the mouth of the Moche River. It was the biggest city of ancient Peru. Far from the granite of the Andes, Chan Chan was constructed with adobe (bricks made from sun-baked mud). The city was laid out in a grid pattern, with 12m-high compound walls marking out the homes of royalty, nobles and craftworkers.

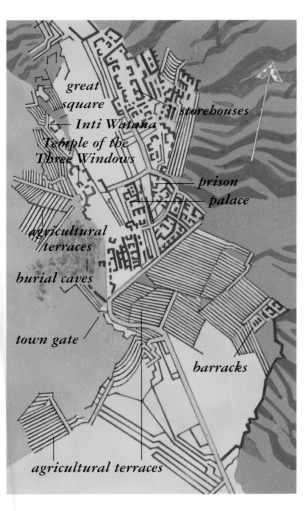

great square

storehouses

Inti Watana

Temple of the Three Windows

prison

palace

agricultural terraces

burial caves

town gate

barracks

agricultural terraces

LIVING IN THE CLOUDS

The small but spectacular Inca town of Machu Picchu clings to a high mountain ridge beneath the peak of Wayna Picchu. In about 1450, it had its own ceremonial square, temples and burial caves. The town also had army barracks, public stores, a prison, housing for craft workers and farmers, and a palace for visiting royalty. The town was defended from attack by a twin wall and a ditch.

A PLAN OF THE TOWN

The long and narrow layout of Machu Picchu was decided by its ridge-top location at 2,743m above sea level. The great square was the religious and political centre of town.

An Inca House

A TYPICAL HOUSE in an Inca town such as Machu Picchu was built from blocks of stone. White granite was the best, being very hard and strong. The roof of each house was pitched at quite a steep angle, so that heavy mountain rains could drain off quickly. Timber roof beams were lashed to stone pegs on the gables, and supported a wooden frame. This was thatched with a tough grass called *ichu*.

Most houses had just one storey, but a few had two or three, joined by rope ladders inside the house or by stone blocks set into the outside wall. Most had a single doorway hung with cloth or hide, and some had an open window on the gable end.

Each building was home to a single family and formed part of a compound. As many as half a dozen houses would be grouped around a shared courtyard. All the buildings belonged to families who were members of the same *ayllu*, or clan.

MUD AND THATCH
Various types of houses were to be seen in different parts of the Inca Empire. Many were built in old-fashioned or in regional styles. These round and rectangular houses in Bolivia are made of mud bricks (adobe). The houses are thatched with *ichu* grass.

upper storey

inside hearth

courtyard

FLOATING HOMES
These houses are built by the Uru people, who fish in Lake Titicaca and hunt in the surrounding marshes. They live on the lake shore and also on floating islands made of matted *totora* reeds. Their houses are made of *totora* and *ichu* grass. Both these materials would have been used in the Titicaca area in Inca times. The reeds are collected from the shallows and piled on to the floor of the lake. New reeds are constantly added.

PICTURES AND POTTERY

Houses with pitched roofs and windows appear as part of the decoration on this pottery from Pacheco, Nazca. To find out about houses in ancient Peru, historians look at surviving towns and ruins, at housing styles still in use today and at old pictures and designs on objects.

SQUARE STONE, ROUND PEG

Squared-off blocks of stone are called ashlars. These white granite ashlars make up a wall in the Inca town of Pisaq. They are topped by a round stone peg. Pegs like these were probably used to support roof beams or other structures, such as ladders from one storey to another.

gable

roofbeam

roof peg

wall niche

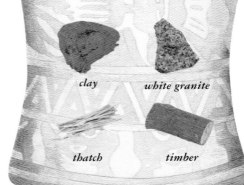

BUILDING MATERIALS

The materials used to build an Inca house depended on local supplies. Rock was the favourite material. White granite, dark basalt and limestone were used when possible. Away from the mountains, clay was made into bricks and dried hard in the sun to make adobe. Roof beams were formed from timber poles. Thatch was made of grass or reed.

clay

white granite

thatch

timber

BUILDING TO LAST

The Incas built simple, but solid, dwellings in the mountains. The massive boulders used for temples and fortresses are here replaced by smaller, neatly cut stones. See how the roof beams are lashed to the gables to support the thatch. Stone roofs were very rare, even on the grandest houses. Timber joists provide an upper storey. The courtyard is used just as much as the inside of the house for everyday living.

Inside the Home

Let's visit the home of an Inca mountain farmer. The outer courtyard is busy, with smoke rising from cooking pots into the fresh mountain air. An elderly woman stacks firewood, while her daughter sorts out bundles of alpaca wool. A young boy brings in a pot of fresh water, splashing the ground as he puts it down.

Pulling aside the cloth at the doorway, you blink in the dark and smoky atmosphere. Cooking has to be done indoors when the weather is poor. The floor of beaten earth is swept clean. There is no furniture at all, but part of the stone wall juts out to form a bench. In one corner there is a clutter of pots and large storage jars. Cloaks and baskets hang from stone pegs on the wall. Niches, inset in the wall, hold a few precious objects and belongings, perhaps a pottery jar or some shell necklaces. Other items include a knife and equipment for weaving or fishing.

POT STOVES

Cooking stoves of baked clay, very like these, have been used in Peru for hundreds of years. Round cooking pots were placed on top of these little stoves. The fuel was pushed in through a hole in the side. Pot stoves are easily carried and can be used outside. Inside the house, there might be a more permanent hearth, made of clay or stone.

DRINK IT UP!

The shape of this two-handled jar and its simple colouring are typically Inca, but the geometric patterns suggest it may have been the work of a Chimú potter. A jar like this might have been used to carry *chicha* (maize beer) made by the *mamakuna* for one of the great religious festivals. People drank far too much *chicha* on these occasions, and drunkenness was common.

INSIDE STORY

What was it like to live in Machu Picchu 500 years ago? The insides of the remaining buildings give us many clues. Even though the thatched roofs and timbers have been lost over the years, some have been restored. Well over half the buildings in Machu Picchu were homes for ordinary people.

REED MATTING

Totora reed matting, used by the Uru people today, is rolled up in bales by Lake Titicaca. In Inca times, reed mats were used as bedding by most people. They slept fully dressed on the ground. Even the emperor and the nobles slept on the floor, but they had blankets and rugs of the finest cloth to cover themselves. Like the Incas, the Uru people have many household uses for *totora* reed. It is a fuel, its flower is used to make medicines and some parts of it may be eaten.

HOUSEHOLD GOURDS

Decorated gourds are still sold in the highlands of Peru. Gourds are pumpkin-like plants bearing fruits with a hard shell. Gourds were often hollowed out and dried and used by the Incas as simple containers for everyday use around the house. They served as water bottles or pots.

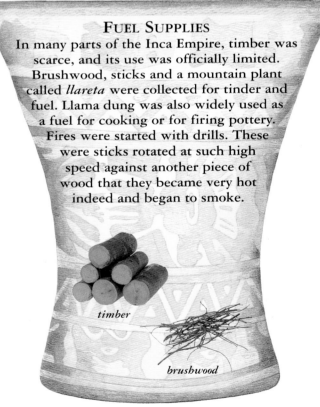

FUEL SUPPLIES

In many parts of the Inca Empire, timber was scarce, and its use was officially limited. Brushwood, sticks and a mountain plant called *llareta* were collected for tinder and fuel. Llama dung was also widely used as a fuel for cooking or for firing pottery. Fires were started with drills. These were sticks rotated at such high speed against another piece of wood that they became very hot indeed and began to smoke.

timber

brushwood

Hunting and Fishing

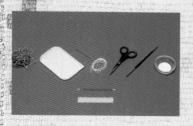

THE INCAS hunted wild animals for sport as well as for food. Every four years, there was a great public hunt, at which beaters would form a line many kilometres long and comb the countryside for game. The hunters closed in on the animals with dogs. Dangerous animals were hunted, such as bears and pumas (South American cougars or mountain lions), as well as important sources of food such as deer, guanaco (a wild relative of the llama) and partridges. After the hunt, the meat was cut into strips and dried in the sun. Hunting was a pastime of royalty and nobles, but ordinary people could hunt with permission. Every child learned how to use a sling – ideal for killing small birds. Nets were used to catch wildfowl on lakes and marshes. Spears, clubs, bows and arrows were also used.

BEAK AND TACKLE
The Moche fisherman shown on this jar is using a pelican to catch fish for him with its great pouch of a beak. Fishing crews of the coast used cotton lines, fish hooks of copper or bone, harpoons, or cotton nets with gourd floats.

SPEARS OF THE NAZCA
A painting on a pottery vase shows two hunters attacking vicuña with spears. It dates from the Nazca civilization, which lasted from about 200BC to AD750. The first Peruvians lived by hunting, but the Inca State depended mainly on farming and fishing for its food. Hunting had become a pastime.

BEYOND THE SURF
A fishing boat made of bound *totora* reed is steered towards the surf at Huancacho, to the north of Trujillo on Peru's north coast. This sight would have been much the same in the days of the Inca Empire. The first view Spanish explorers had of the Inca Empire was of fishing boats and rafts at sea.

A REED BOAT
You will need: dry straw or hay, scissors, ruler, strong thread or twine, pencil, darning needle, plastic lid, PVA glue, paintbrush.

1 Take a fistful of straw or hay and gather it together as shown. Trim one end to make a bundle 20cm long. Make another 20cm bundle and two more 18cm long.

2 Tie a length of thread or twine around one end of a bundle. Then wind it along at 3cm intervals. Bind to a point at one end and tie a knot.

3 Gently bend the bound bundle into a banana shape. Tie and bend the remaining three bundles in exactly the same way. Keep the thread tight.

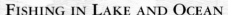

A DAY'S FISHING

Two Moche fishermen sit on a sea-going raft, drinking beer and arguing, no doubt, about the "fish that got away". Fishing was already a major occupation on the Peruvian coast about 4,500 years ago. Later coastal peoples, such as the Chimú, specialized as fishermen, supplying the inland cities with their catches. In Inca times, freshly caught fish from the coast were hurried by special messenger to the royal palace at Cuzco.

FISHING IN LAKE AND OCEAN

The cool currents that sweep up the west coast of Peru provide some of the best fishing in all the Pacific Ocean. Small fish such as sardines and anchovies swarm through these waters. Larger fish and shellfish may also be taken. Inland lakes such as Lake Titicaca are also a rich source of fish.

sardines

anchovies

THE CHASE

A picture painted on a *kero* (wooden beaker), shows an Inca hunter bringing down a guanaco. His weapon is the *bola*, a heavy cord weighted with three balls. It was hurled at a guanaco's legs in order to tangle it. The *bola* was also in Argentina in the 1800s cowboys called *gauchos*.

The curving sides and pointed prow of a reed boat were designed to cut through the waves.

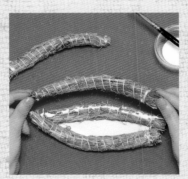

4 Draw a boat shape on plastic, 14cm long, 6cm at the widest point and 4cm wide at the stern. Cut it out. Prick holes 1cm apart around the edge as shown.

5 Thread the needle and carefully sew one of the shorter bundles to one side of the boat. Repeat on the other side of the boat with the matching bundle.

6 Use PVA glue to fix the longer straw or hay bundles on top of the first ones. Curve the uncut ends upwards slightly to form the prow of the boat.

7 Paint the hull of the boat with glue to make it waterproof. Leave it to dry completely before testing your sea-going craft in a bowl of water!

Living on the Land

FREEZE-DRIED POTATOES
A woman of the Tinqui people lays out potatoes on the ground, just as farmers would have done in the days of the Incas. Over two hundred potato varieties were grown in the Andes. They were preserved by being left to dry in the hot daytime sun and cold overnight frosts. Dried, pressed potato, called *chuño*, just needed to be soaked to be ready for cooking.

THE MOUNTAINS, windy plateaus and deserts of Peru are very difficult to farm. Over thousands of years, humans struggled to tame these harsh landscapes. They brought water to dry areas, dug terraced fields out of steep slopes and improved wild plants such as the potato until they became useful food crops. In Inca times, two-thirds of the farmers' produce was set aside for the emperor and the priests, so there was little personal reward for the people who did the hard work.

Royal officials decided the borders of all the fields and of the pastures for llama and alpaca herds. The soil was broken with hoes and plough-like spades called *takllas*. These simple tools were made of hardened wood. Some were tipped with bronze. The Incas knew how to keep the soil well fertilized, using llama dung in the mountains and guano (seabird droppings) on the coast. In dry areas, the Incas built reservoirs called *qochas* to catch the rain. They were experts at irrigation, carefully controlling water-flow through the fields.

A HIGHLAND CROP
Quinua ripens in the sun. This tough crop can be grown at over 3,800m above sea-level, and can survive both warm days and cold nights. *Quinua* was ideal for the Andes. Its seeds were boiled to make a kind of porridge, and its leaves could be stewed as well.

A SAFE HARVEST
The farmer uses his sling to scare hungry birds from the new maize, while his wife harvests the crop. March was the month when the maize ripened, and April was the month of harvest.

AN ANCIENT PATTERN

Painstaking work over many years created these terraced fields, or *andenes*, near the Inca town of Pisaq. All the soil had to be brought up in baskets from the valley floor far below. Terracing aims to provide a workable depth of level soil, while retaining walls prevent earth being washed away by the rains. The base of each terrace was laid with gravel for good drainage. The Pisaq fields belonged to the emperor and produced maize of the highest quality.

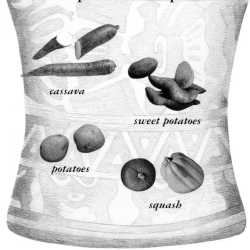

ALL-AMERICAN CROPS

Crops that were once grown in just one part of the world are now grown in other continents as well. Many of the world's most common crops were first grown in the Americas. These include potatoes, tomatoes, maize (sweetcorn), cassava, sweet potatoes and squash.

cassava

sweet potatoes

potatoes

squash

MOTHER EARTH

This gold plate, made by the Chimú people, shows the Earth goddess surrounded by Peruvian crops, each grouped according to its growing season. They include maize, sweet potato and cassava. The Earth goddess was called Pachamama, and she played an especially important part in the religious beliefs of farming villages in the Andes. Most farmers in the Inca Empire spent their lives trying to tame a hostile environment. The fertility of the land was important in religious as well as economic terms.

Food and Feasts

A REGIONAL GOVERNOR might entertain a royal visitor with a banquet of venison (deer meat), roast duck, fresh fish from the lakes or the ocean, and tropical fruits such as bananas and guavas. Honey was used as a sweetener.

Peasants ate squash and other vegetables in a stew, and fish was also eaten where it was available. Families kept guinea pigs for their meat, but most of their food was vegetarian. The bulk of any meal would be made up of starchy foods. These were prepared from grains such as maize or *quinua*, or from root crops such as potatoes, cassava or a highland plant called *oca*. A strong beer called *chicha* was made from maize. The grains were chewed and spat out, then left to ferment in water.

MIXED SPICES

This pottery pestle and mortar may have been used for grinding and mixing herbs. It is about 1,000 years old and was made by the Chimú people. Peruvian dishes were often hot and spicy, using eye-watering quantities of hot chilli peppers. Chilli peppers were one of the first food plants to be cultivated. Peppers of various kinds were grown on the coast and foothills.

MEALS AND MANNERS

Inca nobles ate and drank from wooden plates and painted beakers called *keros*. These continued to be made after the Spanish conquest. Pottery was also used to make beautiful cups and dishes. Most peasants drank and ate from gourds. There were no tables, so food was eaten sitting on the ground. Two main meals were eaten each day, one in the morning and one in the evening.

BEAN STEW

You will need: 250g dried haricot beans, 4 tomatoes, 500g pumpkin, 2 tablespoons paprika, mixed herbs, salt, black pepper, 100g sweetcorn, bowl, large and medium saucepans, knife, chopping board, measuring jug, spoon.

1 Wash the beans in plenty of cold water. Place them in a large bowl and cover them with cold water. Leave them to soak for 3 or 4 hours.

2 Drain the beans and put them in a large saucepan. Cover them with cold water. Bring to the boil. Simmer for 2 hours or until just tender.

3 While the beans are cooking, chop the tomatoes finely on the chopping board. Peel the pumpkin and cut the flesh into 2cm cubes.

A TROPICAL MENU

The mountains were cool because they were high. Down on the lowlands it was much hotter, and tropical crops could be grown wherever there was enough water. These included tomatoes, avocado pears, beans, pumpkin-like squashes, chilli peppers, peanuts and fruits such as guava.

avocado pear

chilli pepper

peanuts

beans

CORN ON THE COB

This maize plant was crafted in Inca silver. The real maize crop would have been almost as precious. Maize could be ground into the flour we call cornmeal, and this was used to make porridge, pancake-like bread and dumplings. The yellow sweetcorn could also be toasted, boiled or puffed up into popcorn.

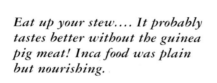

Eat up your stew…. It probably tastes better without the guinea pig meat! Inca food was plain but nourishing.

TO THE LORD OF MAIZE

This maize left in a pottery dish in a Nazca grave is an offering to the Lord of the Maize. Maize played such an important part in the life of Central and South America that it had its own gods, goddesses and festivals.

4 Heat 100ml water in a medium saucepan. Stir in the paprika and bring to the boil. Add the tomatoes and a sprinkling of herbs, salt and pepper.

5 Simmer for 15 minutes until thick and well blended. Drain the beans and return to the large pan with the pumpkin and the tomato mixture. Stir well.

6 Simmer for 15 minutes. Add the sweetcorn and simmer for 5 more minutes until the pumpkin has almost disintegrated and the stew is thick.

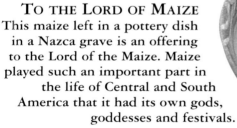

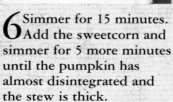

7 Taste (but be careful it's hot!). Add more salt and pepper if necessary. Serve in bowls. Cornbread or tortillas would be an ideal accompaniment.

Textiles and Tunics

IN ALL THE CIVILIZATIONS of the Andes, spinning and weaving were the main household tasks of women of all ranks. Girls learned to weave at an early age, and men wove too. There was a long tradition of embroidery, using bone needles. In Inca times, weaving reached an incredibly high standard. Weaving textiles formed part of the labour tax, like farming or building. Woven cloth was stored in government warehouses and used to pay troops and officials.

Inca men wore a loincloth around the waist, secured by a belt. Over this was a simple knee-length tunic, often made of alpaca wool. On cold nights, they might wear a cloak as well. Women wrapped themselves in a large rectangular cloth of alpaca wool, with a sash around the waist and a shawl. There were many kinds of regional headdresses, caps of looped wool, headbands, hats and feathers. Sandals were made of leather or woven grasses.

INCA FASHION
About 500 years ago, this fine tunic belonged to an Inca nobleman from the south coast of Peru. Its design is simple, but it is beautifully decorated with flower and animal designs. Dress was a status symbol in the Inca Empire. The shape of clothes was much the same for all social classes, but the more important you were, the finer the cloth and the decoration.

PINNED IN STYLE
A long decorative pin called a *tupu* was used by the Incas to fasten dresses and shawls. It might be made from copper, silver or gold. This *tupu* was found at the Sacsahuaman fortress in Cuzco.

AN INCA TUNIC
You will need: blue felt 65cm x 160 cm, red felt 40cm square, PVA glue, brush, tape measure, scissors, ruler, pencil, thread or wool, needle, cream calico fabric, acrylic or fabric paints, paintbrush, water pot.

1 Place the blue felt flat on the table. Position the red felt in the centre of it to form a diamond shape. Glue the red felt carefully in place.

2 For the neck opening, cut a slit 22cm long through the centre of both layers of material as shown, with the long side of the blue felt towards you.

3 Fold the tunic in half along the slit. Halfway along the slit, cut a 12cm slit at right angles to the first. Only cut through one double layer of fabric.

FIBRES AND DYES

Highland animals provided warm woollen fibres. Llamas had the coarsest wool, and vicuñas the softest. Alpaca wool was the one most commonly used. Cotton was grown in the hot lowland regions and was widely worn for its coolness. Plants were used to dye either the yarn or the finished textiles. A scarlet dye called cochineal was obtained from the dried bodies of insects.

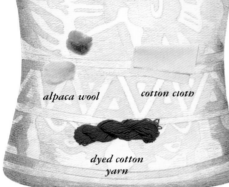

alpaca wool   *cotton cloth*

dyed cotton yarn

SHIMMERING GOLD

For a religious festival, Inca nobles and priests might wear spectacular costumes. This is part of a tunic made of woven alpaca wool decorated with fine gold work. It comes from Peru's south coast. Clothes like these were produced by craftsmen in special workshops. One Chimú tunic was studded with no fewer than 13,000 pieces of gold!

Many Inca tunics were brightly coloured and decorated with geometric patterns.

BACKSTRAPPERS

This Moche painting shows people weaving with backstrap looms. The upright or warp threads are tensioned between an upright post and a beam attached to the weaver's waist. The cross or weft threads are passed in between. Backstrap looms are still used in Central and South America today.

4 Using the coloured thread or wool, sew together the sides of the tunic with large stitches. Leave enough space for armholes at the top.

5 Draw plenty of 5cm squares in pencil on the cream fabric. Paint them in colourful, geometric Inca designs. Look at the patterns here for ideas.

6 Allow the paint to dry completely. Then carefully cut out the squares and arrange them in any pattern you like on the front of your tunic.

7 When you have a pattern you are happy with, glue the squares in position. Wait until the glue is dry before trying on your unique Inca tunic.

Jewels and Feathers

FESTIVAL COSTUMES in the Andes today come in dazzling pinks, reds and blues. In the Inca period it was no different. People loved to wear brightly coloured braids, threads and ribbons. Sequins, beads, feathers and gold were sewn into fabric, while precious stones, red shells, silver and gold were made into beautiful earplugs, necklaces, pendants, nostril-rings and discs. However, it was only the nobles who were allowed to show off by wearing feathers, jewels and precious metals. Some of the most prized ornaments were gifts from the emperor for high-ranking service in the army.

Much of the finest craftwork went into making small statues and objects for religious ceremonies, temples and shrines. During the Inca period, craftworkers were employed by the State. They produced many beautiful treasures, but some of the best of these were the work of non-Inca peoples, particularly the Chimú. Treasures shipped to Spain after the Conquest astounded the Europeans by their fine craftsmanship.

PLUMES OF THE CHIEF
An impressive headdress like this would have belonged to a high-ranking Inca official or general in northern Chile over 500 years ago. The hat is made from coils of dyed llama wool. It is decorated with bold designs, and topped by a spray of feathers.

A SACRED PUMA
This gold pouch in the shape of a puma, a sacred animal, was made by the Moche people between 1,300 and 1,700 years ago. It may have been used to carry *coca* leaves. These were used as a drug during religious ceremonies. The pattern on the body is made up of two-headed snakes.

A GOLD AND SILVER NECKLACE
You will need: self-drying clay, cutting board, ruler, large blunt needle, gold and silver paint, paintbrush, water pot, card, pencil, scissors, strong thread.

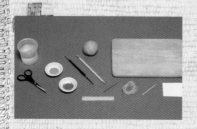

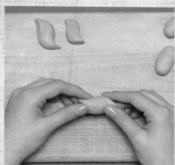

1 Form pieces of clay into beads in the shape of monkey nuts. You will need 10 large beads (about 3.5cm x 2cm) and 10 smaller beads (about 2.5cm x 1.5cm).

2 Use the needle to mark patterns on the beads, so that they look like nut shells. Then carefully make a hole through the middle of each bead. Leave to dry.

3 Paint half the shells of each size gold and half of them silver. You should have 5 small and 5 large gold beads, and 5 small and 5 large silver beads.

PRECIOUS AND PRETTY

The most valued stone in the Andes was blue-green turquoise. It was cut and polished into beads and discs for necklaces, and inlaid in gold statues and masks. Blue lapis lazuli, black jet and other stones also found their way along trading routes. Colombia, on the northern edge of the Inca Empire, mined many precious stones and metals. Seashells were cut and polished into beautiful beads.

emerald   turquoise

lapis lazuli

BIRDS OF A FEATHER

Birds and fish decorate this feather cape. It was made by the Chancay people of the central Peruvian coast between the 1300s and 1500s. It would have been worn for religious ceremonies. Feather work was a skilled craft in both Central and South America. In Inca times, the brilliantly coloured feathers of birds called macaws were sent to the emperor as tribute from the tribes of the Amazon forests.

Necklaces made of gold, silver and jewels would only have been worn by Inca royalty, perhaps the Quya herself.

TREASURE LOST AND FOUND

A beautifully made gold pendant created in the Moche period before the Incas rose to power. After the Spanish conquest of Peru, countless treasures were looted from temples or palaces by Spanish soldiers. Gold was melted down or shipped back to Europe. A few items escaped by being buried in graves. Some have been discovered by archaeologists.

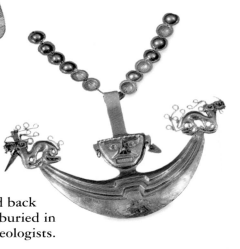

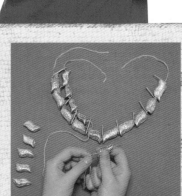

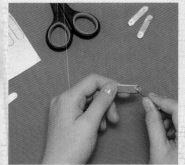

4 Paint some card gold on both sides. On it draw 11 rectangles (3cm x 1cm) with rounded ends. Cut them out and carefully prick a hole in each end.

5 Thread the needle and make a knot 10cm from the end of the thread. Then thread the card strips and large beads alternately, using the gold beads first.

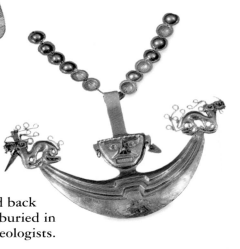

6 Be sure to start and end with card strips. When you have finished, knot the thread tightly next to the last card strip. Cut the thread 10cm from the knot.

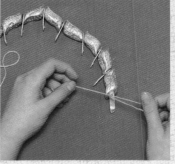

7 Repeat steps 5 and 6 using more thread and the small beads, so that the beads are joined as shown. Finally, knot the ends of the two threads together.

97

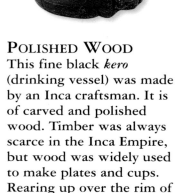

Everyday Crafts

Many beautiful objects produced in the Inca Empire were not made of gold and jewels but of simpler, more down-to-earth materials. Baskets and reed mats were made in early prehistoric times by plaiting and twining various materials. All kinds of small objects, such as bowls, pins, spoons and figures, were carved from bone, stone and wood.

Pottery was being made in Peru by about 2000BC, rather later than in the lands to the north and east. It had a great effect on the way people lived because it affected the production, storage, transportation and cooking of food.

South American potters did not shape their pots on a wheel. They built them up in layers from coils of clay. The coils were smoothed out by hand or with tools, marked or painted, dried in the sun and then baked hard.

Many of the pre-Incan civilizations of the Andes produced beautiful pottery. The Nazca often used bold geometric patterns, while the Moche loved to make jars in the shape of animals and people. Many pots were specially made for religious ceremonies.

POLISHED WOOD
This fine black *kero* (drinking vessel) was made by an Inca craftsman. It is of carved and polished wood. Timber was always scarce in the Inca Empire, but wood was widely used to make plates and cups. Rearing up over the rim of the beaker is a fierce-looking big cat, perhaps a puma or a jaguar.

MODELLED FROM CLAY
A fierce puma bares his teeth. He was made from pottery between AD500 and 800. The hole in his back was used to waft clouds of incense during religious ceremonies in the city of Tiwanaku, near Lake Titicaca.

A TIWANAKU POTTERY JAGUAR
You will need: chicken wire, wire-cutters, ruler, newspaper, scissors, PVA glue, masking tape, flour, water, card, paint, water pot, paintbrush.

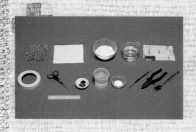

1 Cut a rectangle of chicken wire about 14cm long and 20cm wide. Carefully wrap it around to form a sausage shape. Close one end neatly.

2 Squeeze the other end of the sausage to form the jaguar's neck and head. Fold over the wire at the end to make a neat, round shape for his nose.

3 Make rolls of newspaper about 2.5cm long to form the jaguar's legs. Use strips of paper and glue to join them securely to the jaguar's body as shown.

PRETTY POLLY

This pottery jar, like many from Peru, comes with a handle and a spout. It is shaped and painted to look like a parrot and was made, perhaps 1,000 years before the Incas, by the Nazca potters of southern Peru.

WATER OF LIFE

This Inca bottle is carved with a figure inside a tower collecting water. No community could survive very long without a good supply of fresh water. Many pots, bottles and beakers from the South American civilizations are decorated with light-hearted scenes of everyday activities. They give us a vivid idea of how people used to live.

IN THE POTTER'S WORKSHOP

The potter needed a good supply of sticky clay and plenty of water. He also needed large supplies of firewood or dung for fuel. The potter would knead the clay until it was soft and workable. Sometimes he would mix in sand or crushed shells from the coast to help strengthen the clay. Colours for painting the pottery were made from plants and minerals.

shells   *sand*

clay

The handle and spout design of your Tiwanaku jaguar is known as a stirrup pot, because the arrangement looks rather like the stirrup of a horse.

4 Mix the flour and water to a paste. Use it to glue a layer of newspaper strips all over the jaguar's body. Allow this layer to dry. You will need 3 layers.

5 Cut ears from card. Fix on with masking tape. Tape on rolls of newspaper to make the handle, spout and tail as in the finished pot above.

6 Leave the model in a warm and airy place to dry. Then paint it all over with reddish brown paint. Allow the paint to dry completely.

7 Use black paint and a fine brush to decorate the jaguar as shown in the picture. When the paint is dry, varnish with PVA glue if you wish.

Metals and Mining

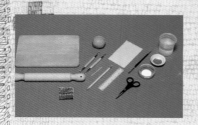

THE WHOLE REGION of the Andes had a very long history of metalworking. A stone bowl that was discovered in the Andahuaylas Valley was nearly 3,500 years old. It contained metalworking equipment and finely beaten gold foil. Braziers found at the town of Machu Picchu, from the end of the Inca period, included traces of molten metal.

The Incas often referred to gold as "sweat of the Sun" and to silver as "tears of the Moon". These metals were sacred not only to the gods but also to their descendants on Earth, the *Sapa Inca* and the *Quya*. At the Temple of the Sun in Cuzco, there was a whole garden made of gold and silver, with golden soil, golden stalks of maize and golden llamas. Imagine how it must have gleamed in the sunshine. Copper, however, was used by ordinary people. It was made into cheap jewellery, weapons and everyday tools. The Incas' love of gold and silver eventually led to their downfall, for it was rumours of their fabulous wealth that lured the Spanish to invade the region.

A SICAN LORD
A ceremonial knife with a crescent-shaped blade is called a *tumi*. Its gold handle is made in the shape of a nobleman or ruler. He wears an elaborate headdress and large discs in his ears. It was made between 1100 and 1300. The knife is in the style of the Sican civilization, which grew up after the decline of the Moche civilization in the AD700s.

A CHIMÚ DOVE
Chimú goldsmiths, the best in the Empire, made this plump dove. When the Incas conquered Chimor in 1470, they forced many thousands of skilled craftsmen from the city of Chan Chan to resettle in the Cuzco area and continue their work.

A TUMI KNIFE
You will need: card, ruler, pencil, scissors, self-drying clay, cutting board, rolling pin, modelling and cutting tools, PVA glue, gold paint, paintbrush, water pot, blue metallic paper.

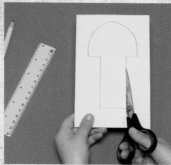

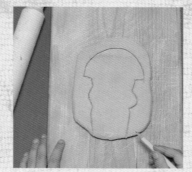

1 On card, draw a knife shape as shown and cut it out. The rectangular part should be 9cm x 3.5cm. The rounded part is 7cm across and 4.5cm high.

2 Roll out a slab of clay about 1cm thick. Draw a *tumi* shape on it as shown. It should be 12.5cm long and measure 9cm across the widest part at the top.

3 Use the cutting tool to cut around the shape you have drawn. Carefully take away the leftover clay. Make sure the edges are clean and smooth.

MINERAL WEALTH

To this day, the Andes are very rich in minerals. The Incas worked with gold, silver, platinum and copper. They knew how to make alloys, which are mixtures of different metals. Bronze was made by mixing copper and tin. However, unlike their Spanish conquerors, the Incas knew nothing of iron and steel. This put them at a disadvantage when fighting the Europeans.

copper   silver

gold

PANNING FOR GOLD

A boy labourer in modern Colombia pans for gold. Some Inca gold was mined, but large amounts also came from panning mountain rivers and streams in the Andes. The river bed was loosened with sticks, and then the water was sifted through shallow trays in search of any flecks of the precious metal that had been washed downstream.

INCA FIGURES

Small ritual figures of women and men from about 6cm high were often made in the Inca period. They were hammered from sheets of silver and gold and were dressed in miniature versions of adult clothing. They have been found on mountain-top shrine sites in the south-central Andes, in carved stone boxes in Lake Titicaca and at important temples.

The Chimú gold and turquoise tumi *was used by priests at religious ceremonies. It may have been used to kill sacrifices.*

4 Cut a slot into the bottom edge of the clay shape. Lifting it carefully, slide the knife blade into the slot. Use glue to make the joint secure.

5 Use a modelling tool to mark the details of the god on to the clay. Look at the finished knife above to see how to do this. Leave everything to dry.

6 When the clay has hardened, paint the whole knife with gold paint. Leave it to dry completely before painting the other side as well.

7 The original knife was decorated with turquoise. Glue small pieces of blue metallic paper on to the handle as shown in the picture above.

Gods and Spirits

THE FIRST PERUVIANS worshipped nature spirits and creatures such as condors, snakes and jaguars. Later peoples began to believe in gods. Some said the world had been created by the god Wiraqocha, the "old man of the sky". He had made the Sun, Moon and stars, and the other gods. He had carved stone statues and made them live, creating the first humans. Myths tell that he sailed away across the Pacific Ocean.

To the Inca people, the most important god was Inti, the Sun. He was the bringer of warmth and light and the protector of the Inca people. Inti's sister and wife was Mamakilya, the silver Moon goddess. Other gods included Pachamama the Earth goddess, Mamacocha goddess of the sea, Kuychi the Rainbow god and Apu Illapu, god of thunder.

THE GATEWAY GOD
Tiwanaku's 1,400-year-old Gateway of the Sun, in Bolivia, is carved from solid rock and is over 3m high. The figure may represent the Chavín Staff god or Wiraqocha. It may be a Sun god, for his headdress is made up of rays.

SPIRITS OF THE MAIZE
On this pottery jar, three gods are shown bursting out of bundles of corn cobs. The jar was made by Moche potters between AD300 and AD700. To all the South American peoples, the world of nature was filled with spiritual forces. They believed that the success of the harvest depended on the good will of the gods.

END OF THE WORLD?
The Incas believed that Inti, the Sun god, dropped into the ocean each evening, swam underneath the Earth and appeared next morning in the east, above the mountains. An eclipse of the Sun was a terrifying experience, a warning that Inti was abandoning the emperor and his people.

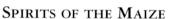

A GOLD SUN GOD MASK
You will need: large piece of card, pencil, ruler, scissors, PVA glue, paintbrush, water pot, gold and black paint.

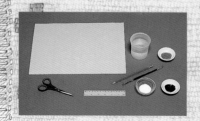

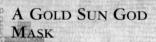

1 Draw the mask shape on card as shown. It should be 60cm wide and 60cm high overall. The side pieces are 40cm high. The narrowest part is 8cm wide.

2 Draw zigzag patterns all around the edge of the mask as shown in the picture above. These patterns represent the powerful rays of the Sun.

3 Carefully cut out the whole mask shape. Then cut out the rays around the edge, making sure you don't snip all the way through by mistake.

ANCIENT SECRETS

A mysterious figure, carved from a great stone pillar, stands amid the ruined temples of Tiwanaku. It holds a banded *kero* or drinking cup in its left hand and a sceptre in its right. Is this the figure of an ancient god? The monument is 7.3m tall and was excavated in 1932. It dates back over 1,500 years, to the days when Tiwanaku became a great religious centre.

A GOLDEN MASK

Gold face-masks were made by several Peruvian peoples, including the Nazca and the Inca. Some were used during festivals in honour of the Sun. Others were laid on the faces of the dead, just as they were in ancient Egypt. This fine mask was made by Moche goldsmiths in about AD400.

Hail to Inti, the Sun god! Your mask looks as if it is made from shining gold, the magical metal of the Sun.

WORSHIPPING THE SUN

A golden face in a sunburst represents Inti, god of the Sun. This picture from the 1700s imagines how the *Coricancha*, the Temple of the Sun, in Cuzco, must have appeared 200 years earlier. It shows the *Sapa Inca* making an offering of maize beer to Inti in the great hall.

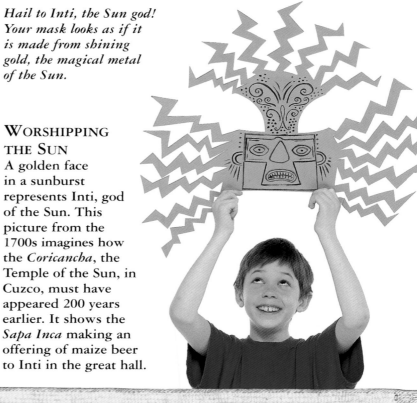

4 Cut out a rectangle of card 15cm x 13cm. Cut a T-shaped piece 14cm across and 11cm high. Also cut out the shapes of eyes, a nose and a mouth.

5 Glue the shapes on to the centre of the mask to form the Sun god's face as shown. Leave the mask flat until the glue is completely dry.

6 Make sure your table top is protected. Cover the whole of the surface of the mask with gold paint. The rays around the edge are fiddly to paint.

7 Finally, use black paint and a fine brush to draw around the face. Add ears and teeth. Decorate the top part with black paint, too.

Festivals and Rituals

THE INCAS loved to celebrate the natural world and its changing seasons. They marked them with special festivals and religious rituals. Some celebrations were held in villages and fields, others took place at religious sites or in the big cities. It is said that the Incas had as many as 150 festivals each year.

The biggest festival of all was *Inti Raymi*, the Feast of the Sun. It was held in June, to mark midwinter in the southern part of the world. *Qapaq Raymi*, the Splendid Festival, was held in December to mark the southern midsummer. This was when boys were recognized as adult warriors, and young nobles received their earplugs. Crop festivals included the Great Ripening each February, Earth Ripening each March and the Great Cultivation each May. The sowing of new maize was celebrated in August. The Feast of the Moon, held in September, was a special festival for women, while the Day of the Dead, in November, was a time to honour one's ancestors.

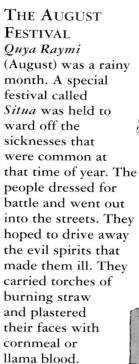

FEAST OF THE SUN
The Quechua people of Peru have revived the ancient festival of *Inti Raymi*. They gather each year at Sacsahuaman fortress, Cuzco, to celebrate the light and warmth of the Sun during the southern midwinter. In Inca times, a golden bowl was raised to the rising Sun. The Sun's rays would be used to make fire.

BRINGER OF RAIN
Drought was feared throughout the Empire, especially in the dry lands of the coast. If rain failed to fall, the life-giving irrigation channels dried up. In desperation, people visited the temples of Apu Illapu, bringer of rain. The priests made offerings and sacrifices, and the pilgrims prayed. The purpose of most Inca ceremonies and festivals was to prevent disaster and to ensure that life carried on.

THE AUGUST FESTIVAL
Quya Raymi (August) was a rainy month. A special festival called *Situa* was held to ward off the sicknesses that were common at that time of year. The people dressed for battle and went out into the streets. They hoped to drive away the evil spirits that made them ill. They carried torches of burning straw and plastered their faces with cornmeal or llama blood.

DANCERS AND MASKS

Drums, music and dance were always an important part of *Inti Raymi*, the Sun Festival. The Incas played rattles and whistles, drums and hand-drums, flutes and panpipes to help them celebrate the festival. Musicians played all day long without taking a break, and some of their ancient tunes are still known. Today, masks representing the Spanish invaders are added to the festivities. The modern festival proves that the old way of life has not been forgotten. Modern Peruvians are proud of their Inca past.

THE EMPEROR'S DAY

The modern festival of *Inti Raymi* attracts thousands to Cuzco. In the days of the Incas, too, nobles poured into the Inca capital from every corner of the Empire. Their aim was to honour the emperor as much as the Sun god. They came carrying tributes from the regions and personal gifts, hoping for the emperor's favour in return.

FIESTA TIME

A drawing from the 1700s shows Peruvian dancers dressed as devils. Many of them are playing musical instruments or carrying long whips. After the conquest, festivals were known by the Spanish term, *fiestas*, and officially celebrated Christian beliefs. However, many of the festivities were still rooted in an Inca past. The dances and costumes often had their origins in Inca traditions.

Flutes, Drums and Dice

A BOY HERDING ALPACAS in the misty fields picks out a tune on a bone whistle. Drums rattle and thump as excited crowds gather in Cuzco for a great festival. The Inca world is full of music.

Music and dance played a very important part in the everyday lives of the Incas. They did not use stringed instruments, but drums and hand-drums, rattles, flutes, whistles and panpipes. Instruments were made from wood, reeds, pottery and bone. At festivals, musicians would play all day without a break. Large bands walked in procession, each panpipe player picking out a different part of the tune. Ancient tunes and rhythms live on in the modern music of the Andes.

The Incas did not have books, but they enjoyed listening to poets and storytellers. They liked tales about the gods, spirits and magic, or princesses and warriors. They enjoyed running races and, like other peoples of the Americas, they loved to gamble. They played games of flicking seeds and rolling dice.

SOUND OF THE PANPIPES
Panpipes made of cane, pottery or bone have been found at many ancient sites in the Inca lands. They are also found in other parts of the world, but their breathy, melodious sound has become very much linked to the Andes. Panpipes are played by blowing across the open end of a sealed tube. They come in many different sizes. In Peru, they are called *antaras* or *zampoñas*.

WHISTLE LIKE A BIRD
A flute is carved to resemble a bird's head and decorated with patterns. It is made from bone and was probably the treasured possession of a Moche musician around AD700.

AN INCA HAND-drum
You will need: card, pencil, ruler, scissors, masking tape, cream calico fabric, PVA glue, paintbrush, paints, water pot, wadding, 30cm length of dowel, coloured wool.

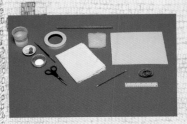

1 Use a pencil and ruler to mark two rectangles, measuring 9cm x 85cm, on the card. Cut them out carefully. They will form the sides of the drum.

2 Bend one rectangle round into a circle and use masking tape to join the ends together. It may be easier to ask a friend to help you do this.

3 Lay the cardboard ring on the calico fabric. Draw a circle around it, leaving a gap of about 2cm. Remove the ring and cut out the fabric circle.

CUZCO DRUMMERS

A modern street band in Cuzco plays the haunting music of the Andes, which has become popular around the world. Local peoples such as the Aymara and Quechua took up new instruments after the Spanish conquest, including various kinds of harp and guitar. However, there are still traces of the Inca musical tradition.

SOUND OF THE CONCH

A Moche noble is shown on a pot made in about AD500. He is blowing a conch at some royal or religious ceremony. Conches are large seashells, which in many parts of the world are blown as trumpets. The Incas called them *wayllakipa*. Conch trumpets were also carried by royal messengers on the Inca roads. They were blown to warn the next relay station they were on the way. Communication was an important part of running the Inca Empire.

Women played hand-drums like this at festivals in Inca times. Drums were sometimes suspended from wooden frames.

4 Paint glue around the edge of the fabric circle. Turn the fabric over. Carefully stretch it over the cardboard ring. Keep it taut and smooth the edges.

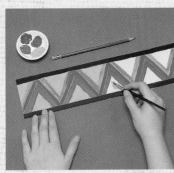

5 Draw a geometric Inca pattern on the remaining strip of card. Use paints to decorate it in bright colours. Lay it flat and leave it to dry.

6 Wrap the painted strip around the drum. Use masking tape to fix one edge to the drum, then use glue to stick down the rest of the patterned strip.

7 Cut out a calico circle 20cm in diameter. Make a beater by wrapping wadding and the calico around one end of the dowel. Tie it with wool.

Medicine and Magic

Like most peoples in the world 500 years ago, the Inca people and their neighbours had some idea of science or medicine. However, curing people was believed to be chiefly a matter of religious rituals and magical spells. No doubt some of these did help people to feel better. Curing sick people was the job either of priests, or of the local healer or medicine man.

As in Europe at that time, Inca healers used fasting and blood-letting (allowing blood to flow from a cut) for many cures. They also tried blood transfusion (putting new blood into someone's body). They succeeded in this far earlier than doctors in other parts of the world, because peoples of the Andes shared the same blood group. The Incas could also set broken bones, amputate limbs, treat wounds and pull teeth. Medicines were made from herbs, roots, leaves and powders.

THE MEDICINE MAN
This Moche healer or priest, from about AD500, seems to be going into a trance and listening to the voices of spirits or gods. He may be trying to cure a sick patient, or he may be praying over the patient's dead body.

MAGIC DOLLS
Model figures like this one, made from cotton and reed, are often found in ancient graves in the Chancay River region. They are often called dolls, but it seems unlikely that they were ever used as toys. They were probably believed to have magical qualities. The Chancay people may have believed that the dolls helped the dead person in another world.

CARRYING COCA
Small bags like these were used for carrying medicines and herbs, especially coca. The leaves of the coca plant were widely used to stimulate the body and to kill pain. Coca is still widely grown in the Andes today. It is used to make the illegal drug cocaine.

MEDICINE BAG
You will need: scissors, cream calico fabric, pencil, ruler, paintbrush, water pot, acrylic or fabric paints, black, yellow, green and red wool, PVA glue, needle and thread, masking tape.

1 Cut two 20cm squares of fabric. Draw a pattern of stripes and diamonds on the fabric and use acrylic or fabric paints to colour them.

2 For the tassels, cut about 10 pieces of wool 8cm long. Fold a piece of wool 15cm long in half. Loop it around each tassel as shown above.

3 Wind a matching piece of wool, 50cm long, around the end of the tassel. When you have finished, knot the wool and tuck the ends inside.

HERBAL REMEDIES

Drugs widely used in ancient Peru included the leaves of tobacco and coca plants. A yellow-flowered plant called calceolaria was used to cure infections. Cinchona bark produced quinine, a medicine we use today to treat malaria. That illness only arrived in South America after the Spanish conquest. However, quinine was used earlier to treat fevers. Suppliers of herbal medicines were known as *hampi kamayuq*.

cinchona tree *tobacco plant*

SKULL SURGERY

Nazca surgeons were able to carry out an operation called trepanation. This involved drilling a hole in the patient's skull in an attempt to relieve pressure on the brain. The Incas believed this released evil spirits. A small silver plate was sometimes fitted over the hole as a protection.

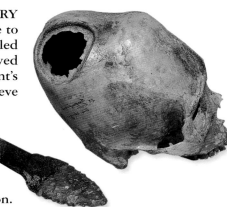

Doctor on call! An Inca medicine chest took the form of a woven bag, carried on the shoulder.

A BAD OMEN

A comet shoots across the night sky. The Incas believed such sights would bring plague or disease in their wake. Other common causes of illness were believed to include witchcraft, evil spirits and a failure to please the gods. People tried to make themselves better by making offerings to the gods at *waq'as* (local shrines). Healers used charms or spells to keep their patients free from evil spirits.

4 Make nine tassels in all. Place them in groups of three along the bottom of the unpainted side of one of the pieces of fabric. Use glue to fix them in place.

5 Allow the glue to dry. Place the unpainted sides of the fabric pieces together. Sew around the edges as shown. Leave the top edge open.

6 Make a strap by plaiting together strands of wool as shown. Cross each outer strand in turn over the middle strand. Tape will help keep the work steady.

7 Knot the ends of the strap firmly. Attach them to both sides of the top of the bag with glue. Make sure the glue is dry before you pick the bag up.

Inca Knowledge

I NCA MATHEMATICIANS used the decimal system, counting in tens. To help with their arithmetic, people placed pebbles or grains of maize in counting frames. These had up to twenty sections. *Quipu* strings were also used to record numbers. Strings were knotted to represent units, tens, hundreds, thousands or even tens of thousands.

The Incas worked out calendars of twelve months by observing the Sun, Moon and stars as they moved across the sky. They knew that these movements marked regular changes in the seasons. They used the calendar to tell them when to plant crops. Inca priests set up stone pillars outside the city of Cuzco to measure the movements of the Sun.

As in Europe at that time, astronomy, which is the study of the stars, was confused with astrology, which is the belief that the stars and planets influence human lives. Incas saw the night sky as being lit up by gods and mythical characters.

FORTUNES FROM THE STARS AND PLANETS
An Inca astrologer observes the position of the Sun. The Incas believed that careful watching of the stars and planets revealed their influence on our lives. For example, the star pattern or constellation that we call the Lyre was known to the Incas as the Llama. It was believed that it influenced llamas and those who herded them.

THE SUN STONE
A stone pillar called *Inti Watana* (Tethering Post of the Sun) stood at the eastern edge of the great square in Machu Picchu. It was like a giant sundial and the shadows it cast confirmed the movements of the Sun across the sky – a matter of great practical and religious importance.

A QUIPU

You will need: scissors, rope and string of various thicknesses, a 90cm length of thick rope, paints, paintbrush, water pot.

1 Cut the rope and string into about 15 lengths measuring from 20cm to 80cm. Paint them in various bright colours. Leave them to dry completely.

2 To make the top part of the *quipu*, take a piece of thick rope, about 90cm long. Tie a knot in each end as shown in the picture above.

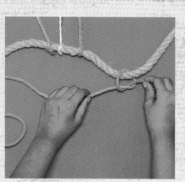

3 Next, take pieces of thinner rope or string of various lengths and colours. Tie them along the thicker rope, so that they all hang on the same side.

THE MILKY WAY

On dark nights, Inca priests looked for the band of stars that we call the Milky Way. They called it *Mayu* (Heavenly River) and used it to make calculations about seasons and weather conditions. In its darker spaces they saw the shadow of the Rain god Apu Illapu. The shape of the Milky Way was believed to mirror that of the Inca Empire.

SUN WATCH

The *Inti Watana* (Tethering Post of the Sun) at Machu Picchu was one of many Sun stones across the Empire. *Sukana* (stone pillars) near Cuzco showed midsummer and midwinter sun positions. The Sun god, Inti, was believed to live in the north and go south each summer.

KEEPERS OF THE QUIPU

Vast amounts of information could be stored on a *quipu*. A large one might have up to 2,000 cords. The *quipu* was rather like an Inca version of the computer, only the memory had to be provided by the operator's brain rather than a silicon chip. Learning the *quipu* code of colours, knots, and major and minor strings took many years. Expert operators were called *quipu-kamayuq*.

You have now designed a simple quipu. Can you imagine designing a system that would record the entire population of a town, their ages, the taxes they have paid and the taxes they owe? The Incas did just that!

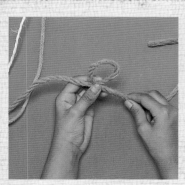

4 Tie knots in the thinner ropes or strings. One knot you might like to try begins by making a loop of rope as shown in the picture above.

5 Pass one end of the rope through the loop. Pull the rope taut but don't let go of the loop. Repeat this step until you have a long knot. Pull it tight.

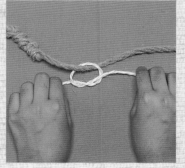

6 Make different sizes of knots on all the ropes or strings. Each knot could represent a family member, school lesson or other important detail.

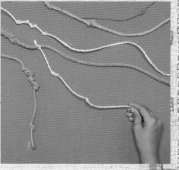

7 Add some more strings to the knotted strings. Your *quipu* may be seen by lots of people. Only you will know what the ropes, strings and knots mean!

Married Life

WEDDINGS WERE SOME of the happiest occasions in an Inca village. They offered a chance for the whole community to take time off work. The day was celebrated with dancing, music and feasting. The groom would probably be 25 years of age, at which point he was regarded as an adult citizen, and his bride would be rather younger – about 20.

For the first year of the marriage, a couple did not have to pay any tax either in goods or labour. However, most of their lives would be spent working hard. When they were elderly, they would still be expected to help with household chores. Later still, when they became too old or sick to look after themselves, they received free food and clothes from the State warehouse. They would then be cared for by their clan or family group.

Not everyone was expected to get married. The *mamakuna* (virgins of the Sun) lived rather like nuns, in a special convent in Cuzco. They wove fine cloth and carried out religious duties. No men were allowed to enter the *mamakuna's* building.

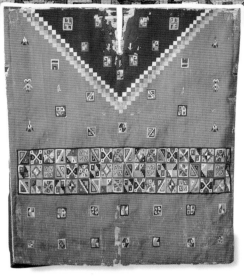

WEDDING CLOTHES
An Inca nobleman would get married in a very fine tunic. This one is from the southern coast of Peru. Commoners had to wear simpler clothes, but couples were presented with free new clothes from the State warehouses when they married.

REAL PEOPLE
This jar from the Moche period is over 1,300 years old. Unlike the portraits on many jars, it seems to show a real person sitting down and thinking about life. It reminds us that ancient empires were made up of individuals who fell in love, raised children and grew old, just as people do today.

MARRIAGE PROSPECTS
Two Inca noble women are painted on the side of this *kero* (wooden beaker). Women of all social classes were only allowed to marry with the approval of their parents and of State officials. They were expected to remain married for life and divorce was forbidden. If either the husband or wife was unfaithful, he or she could face trial and might even be put to death.

A ROYAL MARRIAGE

A prince of the emperor's family marries in Cuzco. The scene is imagined by an artist of the 1800s. An emperor had many secondary wives in addition to his sister-empress. Between them they produced very many princes and princesses. Inca royal families were divided by jealousy and by complicated relations, which often broke out in open warfare. The emperor ordered his officials to keep tight control over who married whom. His own security on the throne depended on it.

A HOME OF THEIR OWN

When a couple married, they left their parents' houses and moved into their own home, like this one at Machu Picchu. The couple now took official control of the fields they would work. These had been allocated to the husband when he was born. Most couples stayed in the area occupied by their own clan, so their relatives would remain nearby.

HIS AND HERS

The everyday lives of most married couples in the Inca Empire were taken up by hard work. Men and women were expected to do different jobs. Women made the *chicha* beer and did the cooking, weaving and some field work. Men did field work and fulfilled the *mit'a* labour tax in service to the Inca State. They might build irrigation channels or repair roads.

An Inca Childhood

A NEWBORN INCA BABY was immediately washed in cold water and wrapped in a blanket. It was breast-fed at three set times each day, but cuddling was frowned upon.

Babyhood ended with a naming ceremony at the age of two, during which a lock of hair was cut off. The toddler still spent a lot of time playing – spinning tops were a popular toy. From now on, however, both boys and girls would be expected to start helping out around the house.

Girls came of age at 14. Royal officials decided whether they would become *akllakuna*. Those selected went for training in Cuzco, while the rest remained in their villages. Boys also came of age at 14 and were given a loincloth as a mark of manhood. Boys from noble families were put through special tests of endurance and knowledge. They were then given the weapons and the earplugs that showed their rank in society.

THREE FOR THE POT

A young Inca has been helping out by herding llamas in the mountains. He has taken a net along and caught some wildfowl in the reeds beside the lake. Contemporary pictures like this show that children and teenagers seem to have led a tough, open-air life.

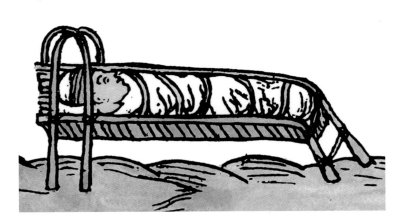

ROCK-A-BYE BABY

At the age of four days, a baby was wrapped up in swaddling clothes and tied into its *quiru* (wooden cradle). This could be placed on the ground and rocked, or tied on the mother's back. After a few months, the baby was taken from the cradle and left in a special pit, which served as a playpen.

HARD TIMES

Children were often punished severely. Even noble children could expect to be beaten by their teacher on the soles of their feet if they didn't work hard. There were laws to protect children from violence and kidnapping, but in times of famine or war children must have suffered dreadfully.

LEARNING TO SPIN YARN

Inca girls were taught to spin using a drop spindle and a distaff, a stick round which they wound the prepared fleece or cotton. Using the right hand they twisted the spindle with its whirling weight attached. They guided the fibres from the distaff with the left hand. The fibre was twisted into yarn, which was used for weaving on a backstrap loom. The hunchbacked woman in this drawing is spinning as she walks along the road. She was trained in her youth to be a useful member of Inca society.

HELPING IN THE FIELDS

This Inca boy has a sling and is attacking the flocks of birds that are robbing the maize fields in his village. Both boys and girls were expected to help with the farming and to learn working skills from their parents, such as weaving or terrace-building. Most children in the Inca Empire did not go to school but were educated by their families. They learned what they needed for adult life and no more. The same was true in most parts of the world 500 years ago.

GOING TO SCHOOL

This building at Laris, near Cuzco is a school. Before the Spanish invasion, there was little formal education in Peru. Teenage boys from noble families were taught in Cuzco. Their timetable included Quechua language in Year One, Inca religion and astronomy in Year Two, arithmetic, geometry and *quipu* studies in Year Three, and history in Year Four. *Quipus* were knotted strings used to record information. Pupils also studied music, poetry and the geography of Tawantinsuyu. The only girls to receive formal education were the *akllakuna*, who were taught weaving, cooking and religious studies.

Land of the Dead

ARCHAEOLOGISTS HAVE FOUND many burial sites in the Andes. Bodies are most easily preserved in very dry or very cold conditions, and this region has both. As early as 3200BC, the Andean peoples learned how to embalm or mummify bodies. The insides were often taken out and buried. The rest of the body was dried, and the eyes were replaced with shells. When an Inca emperor died, his mummified body was kept in his former palace. The body was waited on by his descendants and even taken out to enjoy festivals! Respect for ancestors was an important part of Inca religious beliefs.

FACING THE NEXT WORLD
Many South American mummies were buried in a sitting position. Their knees were drawn up and bound into position with cord. Over their faces were masks of wood, clay or gold, depending on their status. This mask, perhaps from the pre-Incan Nazca period, was decorated with coloured feathers.

Inca funerals were sad occasions with slow music. Women cut off their long hair as a sign of grief. When the emperor died, some of his wives and servants were killed. The Incas believed that good people went to *Hanakpacha*, the Empire of the Sun, after death. Bad people had a wretched afterlife, deep in the Earth.

THE LORD OF SIPÁN
In 1988, a Peruvian archaeologist called Dr Walter Alva opened up a royal tomb at Sipán, near Chiclayo in northern Peru. The "Lord of Sipán" had been buried there with his servants, amid treasures made of gold, silver, copper and precious stones. The tomb belonged to the Moche civilization, which flourished between AD1 and 700.

A CHANCAY GRAVE DOLL

You will need: scissors, cream calico fabric, pencil, ruler, paints, paintbrush, water pot, black wool, PVA glue, wadding, 20 red pipecleaners, red wool.

1 Cut two rectangles of fabric 16cm x 11cm for the body. Cut two shield-shaped pieces 7cm wide and 8cm long for the head. Paint one side as shown.

2 Cut 35 strands of black wool, each 18cm long, for the doll's hair. Glue them evenly along the top of the wrong side of the unpainted face shape.

3 Cut a piece of wadding slightly smaller than the face. Glue it on top of the hair and face below. Then glue the painted face on top. Leave to dry.

TOWERS OF THE DEAD

Various South American peoples left mummies in stone towers called *chullpas*, such as these ones at Nina Marca. Goods were placed in the towers for the dead person to use in the next life. These included food and drink, pins, pots, knives, mirrors and clothes. Discoveries of the goods left in graves have helped archaeologists find out about everyday life long ago.

DEATH WITH HONOUR

This face mask of beaten gold dates back to the 1100s or 1200s, during the Inca Empire. Its eyes are made of emerald, and it is decorated with pendants and a nose ornament. The crest on top, decorated with animal designs, serves as a crown or headdress. This mask was made by a Chimú goldsmith and laid in a royal grave.

FACE OF THE MUMMY

This head belonged to a body that was mummified over 1,400 years ago in the Nazca desert. The skin is leathery, and the mouth gapes open in a lifelike manner. Most extraordinary is the skull's high, domed forehead. This shows that the dead person had his head bound with cloth as a small child. An elongated head was a sign of status amongst the Nazca people.

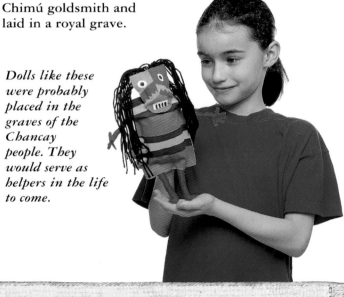

Dolls like these were probably placed in the graves of the Chancay people. They would serve as helpers in the life to come.

4 For each arm, take five pipecleaners and cut them to 11cm. Twist them together to within 1.5cm of one end. Splay this end to make fingers.

5 Make legs in the same way, but this time twist all the way and bend the ends to make feet. Wind wool around the arms and legs to hide the twists.

6 Assemble the doll as in the picture. Use glue to fix the arms and legs and wadding between the body pieces. Glue the front piece of the body in place.

7 Use glue to fix the head to the front of the body, making sure the hair does not become caught. Leave the doll to dry completely before picking it up.

117

Warriors and Weapons

The Inca Empire was brought about and held together by military force. Its borders were defended by a string of forts. The cities served as walled refuges when the surrounding countryside was under attack from enemies. There was a standing army of some 10,000 elite troops, but the great bulk of soldiers were conscripts, paying their State dues by serving out their *mit'a*. Badges and headdresses marked the rank of officers. In the 1500s women joined in the resistance to the Spanish conquest, using slings to devastating effect. The Incas were fierce fighters, but they stood no chance against the guns and steel of the Spanish.

TAKE THAT!
This star may have looked pretty, but it was deadly when whirled from the leather strap. It was made of obsidian, a glassy black volcanic rock. Inca warriors also fought with spikes set in wooden clubs, and some troops favoured the *bolas*, corded weights that were also used in hunting. Slings were used for scaring the birds. However, in the hands of an experienced soldier, they could be used to bring down a hail of stones on enemies and crack their heads open.

WAITING FOR THE CHARGE
A Moche warrior goes down on one knee and brings up his shield in defence. He is bracing himself for an enemy charge. All South American armies fought on foot. The horse was not seen in Peru until the Spanish introduced it.

IN THE BARRACKS
Many towns of the Inca Empire were garrisoned by troops. These restored barrack blocks at Machu Picchu may once have housed conscripted soldiers serving out their *mit'a*. They would have been inspected by a high-ranking general from Cuzco. During the Spanish invasion, it is possible that Machu Picchu became a base for desperate resistance fighters.

AN INCA HELMET
You will need: scissors, cream calico fabric, ruler, balloon, PVA glue, paintbrush, paints, water pot, yellow and black felt, black wool.

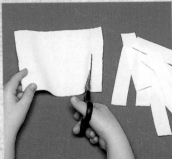

1 Cut the fabric into strips about 8cm x 2cm as shown in the picture. You will need enough to cover the top half of a blown-up balloon three times.

2 Blow up the balloon to the same size as your head. Glue the strips of fabric over the top half. Leave each layer to dry before adding the next.

3 When the last layer is dry, pop the balloon and carefully pull it away. Use scissors to trim round the edge of the helmet. Paint it a reddish orange.

KINGS OF THE CASTLE

The massive fortress of Sacsahuaman at Cuzco was built on a hill. One edge was formed by a cliff and the other defended by massive terraces and zigzag walls. The invading Spanish were excellent castle-builders. They were awestruck by Sacsahuaman's size and defences. The Incas regarded warfare as an extension of religious ritual. Sacsahuaman was certainly used for religious ceremonies. Some historians claim that the Inca capital was laid out in the shape of a giant puma, with Sacsahuaman as its head.

SIEGE WARFARE

An Inca army takes on the enemy at Pukara, near Lake Titicaca. Most South American cities were walled and well defended. Siege warfare was common. The attackers blocked the defenders' ways of escape from the town. After the conquest, in 1536, Inca rebels under Manko Inka trapped Spanish troops in Cuzco and besieged them for over a year.

Inca helmets were round in shape and made of wood or cane. They were decorated with braids and crests.

4 Take the felt. Measure and cut a 3cm yellow square, a yellow circle with a diameter of 3cm, a 9cm yellow square and a 5.5cm black square.

5 Glue the felt shapes on to the helmet as shown above. Glue a 2cm-wide strip of yellow felt along the edge of the helmet to neaten the edge.

6 Take 12 strands of black wool, each 30cm long. Divide them into 3 hanks of 4 strands. Knot the ends together, then plait to the end.

7 Knot the end of the finished braid. Make two more. Glue them inside the back of the helmet. Wait until it is dry before trying it on.

119

Eclipse of the Sun

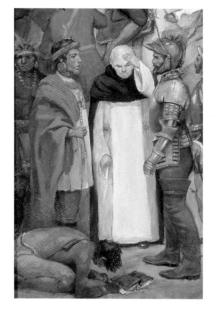

IN NOVEMBER 1532, the emperor Ataw Wallpa met the Spanish invaders, under Francisco Pizarro, in the great square of Cajamarca. The *Sapa Inca* was riding in a litter that was covered in feathers. Surrounding him were troops glinting with gold. The sound of conch trumpets and flutes echoed around the buildings. The Spanish were amazed by the sight, and the Incas looked uneasily at the strangers with their fidgeting horses.

Within just one hour, thousands of Incas had been killed, and their emperor was in the hands of the Spanish. Ataw Wallpa was arrested. He offered to raise a ransom to secure his release. Silver and gold arrived by the tonne, filling up a whole room. The Spanish gained unimagined riches. Even so, in the summer of 1533 they accused Ataw Wallpa of treason, and he was garrotted (executed by strangulation). Resistance to the Spanish continued for another 39 years, but South American civilization had changed for ever that day.

THE WORD OF GOD?
When emperor Ataw Wallpa met the Spanish invaders in Cajamarca, he was approached by a Christian priest called Vincente de Valverde. The priest raised a Bible and said that it contained the words of God. Ataw Wallpa grabbed the book and listened to it. No words came out, so he hurled it to the ground. The Spanish were enraged, and the invasion began.

CONQUEST AND SLAVERY
The Spanish conquest was a disaster for all the native peoples of the Americas. Many of them were murdered, enslaved or worked to death in the mines. The Spanish introduced money into Inca life, trading in silver, gold, farm produce and coca. But it was mostly the Spanish settlers who became wealthy, not the native people.

"SANTIAGO!"
Before the 1532 meeting with Ataw Wallpa in the great square of Cajamarca, the Spanish invader Francisco Pizarro had hidden troops behind buildings. When he shouted the pre-arranged signal of *Santiago!* (St James), they began to shoot into the crowd. Chaos broke out as the emperor was seized and taken prisoner.

TEARS OF THE MOON

In 1545, the Spanish discovered silver at Potosí in the Bolivian Andes and began to dig mines. The wealth was incredible, but the working conditions were hellish. Local people were forced to work as slaves. Mule trains carried the silver northwards to Colombian ports, making Spain the richest country in the world.

DESCENDANTS OF THE EMPIRE

Christians of Quechuan and mixed descent take part in a procession through Cuzco. In the Andes, over the past few hundred years, many Inca traditions, festivals and pilgrimages have become mixed up with Christian ones. Indigenous peoples today make up 45 per cent of the total population in Peru, 55 per cent in Bolivia, and 25 per cent in Ecuador.

THE TREASURE FLEETS

The Spanish plundered the treasure of the Incas and the minerals of the Andes. Big sailing ships called galleons carried the gold and silver back to Europe from ports in Central and South America. The region was known as the Spanish Main. Rival European ships, many of them pirates from England, France and the Netherlands, began to prey on the Spanish fleets. This led to long years of warfare. Between 1820 and 1824, Spain's South American colonies finally broke away from European rule to become independent countries, but most of the region's native peoples remained poor and powerless.

Glossary

A

adobe Sun-dried mud bricks.

ahaw Name given to their rulers by the Maya.

akllakuna Inca girls chosen for special training.

alloy A metal made from a mixture of other metals.

alpaca A llama-like animal, valued for its wool.

amaranth A bushy plant with edible seeds.

amate Paper made from fig-tree bark.

aqueduct A raised channel carrying water supplies.

archaeology The study of ancient remains and ruins.

ashlar A squared-off block of stone, used for building.

astrology The belief that the stars, planets, Sun and Moon influence the way we live.

astronomy The scientific study of the heavens.

atlatl An Aztec spear-thrower.

ayllu An Inca land-holding clan.

B

backstrap loom Equipment for weaving. One end is tied around the weaver's waist.

barter To exchange items for others of similar value.

blood-letting Cutting a patient's veins to let blood flow out, for medical reasons.

bola Three heavy balls tied to cords, used for hunting and as a weapon.

C

calpulli An Aztec family or neighbourhood group.

cassava A starchy edible root, also known as manioc.

causeway A raised roadway.

cenote A holy waterhole.

chacmool A statue shaped like a dying warrior or rain god, used to hold blood or hearts.

chicha Beer made from maize.

chinampa An Aztec garden built on reclaimed land.

chullpa An Inca burial-tower.

chultun An underground tank for storing water.

coca A South American plant used by the Incas as a drug, as medicine, and for fortune-telling.

cochineal A red dye made from crushed beetles.

codex A folding book.

conch A seashell that makes a booming sound when blown.

conscription Forced service to the State.

D

distaff A stick used to hold fibres for spinning.

drop-spindle A hand-held weight used when spinning.

E

empire A group of lands ruled by a single country.

G

glyph A picture-symbol used in Mesoamerican writing.

gourd A hard-skinned plant, hollow when dried, used as a container.

guanaco A wild animal related to the llama.

H

huautli A bush with edible seeds grown in Mesoamerica.

I

incense Gum or other material burned to produce sweet-smelling smoke.

indigenous Native to a country.

inscribed Carved on stone.

irrigation Bringing water to dry lands so crops can be grown.

J

jade A smooth green stone.

K

katun A Maya measurement of time (72,000 days).

kero A drinking vessel.

kuraka An Inca local chief.

L

litter A portable bed.

llama A camel-like animal, kept by Incas for its wool, and sacrificed in religious ceremonies.

loom Equipment for weaving threads to make cloth.

M

macehualtin The Aztec name for ordinary people.

macuahuitl An Aztec war-club.

mahk'ina A Maya ruler.

mamakuna Inca Virgins of the Sun, who stayed unmarried and led religious lives.

manioc A starchy edible root.

mit'a Conscripted workers, forced to work for the Inca State as a way of paying tax.

O

obsidian A black, glassy stone.

ocarina A round, hollow musical instrument, played by blowing.

omen A sign of good or bad fortune in the future.

oracle A person or place that foretells future events.

P

panaka A land-holding group made up of Inca nobles who are related to each other.

panpipes A musical instrument made of pipes joined together.

patolli An Aztec game played with counters.

peccary A South American wild pig.

plumbline A weighted cord, used to measure whether a wall is vertical.

pochteca Aztec merchants.

pulque An Aztec wine made from the maguey cactus.

Q

quetzal A rainforest bird with brightly-coloured, long, green tail-feathers.

quinua A plant with seeds that can be used to make a sort of porridge and whose leaves can be cooked like spinach.

quipu Knotted, coloured cords used by the Inca people to record information.

Quya The Inca empress.

S

Sapa Inca The Inca emperor.

slip Clay mixed with water and used to decorate pottery.

smelt To extract metal from rock by crushing and heating.

stela A tall stone pillar.

stucco Plaster used to cover and decorate buildings.

T

tamales Maize dumplings with a meat or vegetable filling, made in Mesoamerica.

tlachtli The Aztec ball-game.

tlatoani The Aztec name for their ruler.

topos An Inca unit of measurement (around 7km).

tortillas Maize pancakes.

trapezoid Having four sides, of which only two are parallel. Inca windows and doors were often trapezoid.

trepan To bore a hole in someone's skull for medical or religious reasons.

tribute Taxes paid in goods by conquered people.

tumi An Inca ceremonial knife with a semi-circular blade.

tumpline A band of cloth, worn over the shoulders by porters in Mesoamerica, to help them carry heavy loads.

tupu A long pin used by the Incas to fasten women's clothes. The Incas did not have buttons.

U

uictli An Aztec digging stick.

V

vicuna A llama-like animal, whose fine silky wool was used to make the finest cloth.

volador An Aztec religious ritual in which four men spin round and round on a pole.

W

wa'qa An Inca holy place or holy object.

Y

yucca A desert plant with long fleshy leaves.

Index

PICTURE CREDITS

b = bottom, t = top,
c = centre, l = left, r = right